Early American History

A LITERATURE APPROACH FOR INTERMEDIATE GRADES

Early American History: A Literature Approach for Intermediate Grades
by Rea Berg and Rebecca Manor © 2021

Published by Beautiful Feet Books
ISBN 978-1893103900
Layout and Design by Ryan Maloney

Table of Contents

How To Use This Guide

Welcome to the fascinating world of our nation's founding. Covering over a thousand years, this study encompasses Native cultures, the Vikings, the Age of Discovery, colonial settlements, revolution, slavery, civil war, and emancipation. It may seem daunting to cover all this history in a year, but this guide is your tool, designed to educate and delight your student.

Grade Level and Overview: This is a one-year study appropriate for 4th through 6th grade. The heart of this study is reading aloud great literature with your students. Exploring the world through story is often one of the most cherished experiences shared by homeschooling families. The guide is inspired by the Charlotte Mason method of education: reading, reasoning, relating, and recording.

This course can be used for a broad grade range so we want to provide some guidelines for the assignments. For younger students, simply reading, narrating, notebooking, and having discussions about the readings is enough. Older students should begin developing research and writing skills. Being able to combine reading aloud, history, vocabulary, geography, literature, and more is one of the benefits of homeschooling! Writing prompts are provided to encourage the development of research and writing skills. These are just basic recommendations and should be scaled based on the child's age, ability, and learning style. You're the teacher and parent—you know best!

Content: Livy, the ancient Roman historian, said:

> *"What makes the study of history so valuable, is the fact that you can behold, displayed as on a monument, every kind of conduct. Thence you may select for yourself and your country, that which you may imitate, thence note what is shameful in the undertaking, and shameful in the result, which you may avoid."*

As Livy notes so well, there are triumphal and disappointing events in history. While this study introduces hard topics, it does so only with age-appropriate detail, recognizing that as students mature there will be ample opportunity for expanding their knowledge. This gives you, the teacher, the option to choose when that time comes. Topics like slavery and the mistreatment of Native Peoples are covered both for historical accuracy and to help cultivate compassion and empathy. The resources in Rabbit Trails offer curated selections to expand on these topics. **Note:** *Lincoln: A Photobiography* includes two photographs of battleground casualties on pages 88 and 100. These photos are disturbing and teachers may want to consider covering them for younger or sensitive students.

Historical perceptions of unknown or unfamiliar cultures and people change over time as knowledge and respect overcome ignorance and prejudice. This process repeats itself throughout history and is preserved in historical documents and texts. Rewriting and erasing this evidence to suit modern taste does not provide the opportunities for correction and instruction we believe to be such a valuable aspect of learning history. Recognizing human brokenness and seeing the failings of the past is part of the reason we study history and we see the hard parts of it as inescapable and valuable in the lessons they teach. As you read through the literature included in this study you will encounter a few instances where these historical attitudes and descriptions will be offensive. We have provided discussion questions to help you navigate these topics as well as content warnings on specific lessons.

Pace: This study contains 129 lessons; if you are planning on the standard 180-day school year, complete 3-4 lessons each week. If you are teaching younger students or using it across a range of ages, work at your own pace. There is no pre-set schedule. When life gets busy or the holidays are approaching, slow down. If your students are intrigued by a certain subject, follow those rabbit trails. Our guides are designed to support your teaching style, not dictate it. One of the greatest gifts of homeschooling is the flexibility and freedom that is built into setting your own schedule. This teacher guide is designed to be a tool, not a taskmaster.

Activities: This guide includes some recommended hands-on activities. We also link to websites that have further activities. None of these are required. Do what adds enjoyment to your study.

Student Notebook: Each student should have a notebook that they are comfortable working with. We suggest a composition notebook. All written work, coloring pages, reports, and mapping activities will be added to this notebook. At the end of the year, your student's notebook will be a wonderful portfolio of what they've learned.

Picture Packet: Throughout this study you will be referred to the Picture Packet—a free download available via the QR code or on our website: www.bfbooks.com/Info-FAQ/Free-Downloads. These pages are to be printed and copied for use in the student notebook.

Comprehension and Discussion Questions: As you read through the literature with your students, use the questions to help spur conversation and verbal processing, unless you are following a Charlotte Mason narration model. There are some comprehension questions with specific answers provided to check reading comprehension, but one of the main goals of this program is creating conversations. The discussion questions are designed to encourage critical thinking.

Websites: Throughout the study you will find a curated selection of websites. These specific website pages have all been viewed and deemed appropriate and accurate at the time of printing. Potential objectionable material has been noted. The recommendation of one page on a website is not an endorsement of the entire contents of that website. Always use the internet with care and under adult supervision. Simply type in the title as it appears to find the correct information. If a web link is no longer working, don't give up. Simply use the words in the web address to guide your search.

Nature Study: This component enhances the study with images of native birds and animals! These images are included in the downloadable Picture Packet referenced above. Students are instructed to research the animals and record facts in the notebook along with the pictures. Sites like www.allaboutbirds.org, nationalgeographic.com, and www.fws.gov are very helpful.

Rabbit Trails: At the beginning of each section, you will find a list of additional recommended books to check out from your local library. None of these titles are required, we simply provide these lists in order to help you sift through the hundreds of books available on the many topics covered in this study. However, if you have a voracious reader or if a certain topic proves especially interesting, these curated selections will allow your student to choose titles for themselves. This empowers them to develop agency in their own education.

The Historic Table: These sections offer you and your students a fun way to celebrate the completion of each section. We have gathered recipes that are either culturally or historically accurate to give students a taste for the culinary element of history. Some of the recipes are updated to make them more appealing to our twenty-first-century palates. Enjoy!

Do I Have to Do Everything in Every Lesson? No! Again, this is a tool, not a taskmaster. Everything in this guide is provided to make your job easier and save you time. Every lesson, assignment, and activity is here to help you expand the literature, pull out historical content, and provide structure and guidance, but feel free to skip steps when it suits your family.

Lastly, share your work on social media and tag us at **#beautifulfeetbooks**. We love seeing your creativity.

Literature Used In This Study

Resource

A Child's First Book of American History
by Earl Schenck Miers, illustrated by James Daugherty

Indigenous Peoples of North America & First Encounters

People of the Breaking Day
written and illustrated by Marcia Sewall

The Vikings
by Elizabeth Janeway

Hiawatha and the Peacemaker
by Robbie Robertson, illustrated by David Shannon

Children of the Longhouse
by Joseph Bruchac

The Golden Age of Discovery

Where Do You Think You're Going, Christopher Columbus?
by Jean Fritz, illustrated by Margot Tomes

Pedro's Journal
by Pam Conrad, illustrated by Peter Koeppen

The Colonies

Pocahontas and the Strangers
by Clyde Robert Bulla, illustrated by Peter Burchard

The Landing of the Pilgrims
by James Daugherty

The World of William Penn
written and illustrated by Genevieve Foster

Amos Fortune, Free Man
by Elizabeth Yates, illustrated by Nora S. Unwin

The Revolutionary War

A Voice of Her Own: The Story of Phillis Wheatley, Slave Poet
by Kathryn Lasky, illustrated by Paul Lee

George vs. George: The American Revolution as Seen From Both Sides
written and illustrated by Rosalyn Schanzer

Toliver's Secret
by Esther Wood Brady

Why Not, Lafayette?
by Jean Fritz, illustrated by Ronald Himler

Remember the Ladies: A Story About Abigail Adams
by Jeri Chase Ferris, illustrated by Ellen Beier

Shh! We're Writing the Constitution
by Jean Fritz, illustrated by Tomie dePaola

The Young United States

How We Crossed the West: The Adventures of Lewis & Clark
written and illustrated by Rosalyn Schanzer

Heart of a Samurai
by Margi Preus

The Story of Harriet Tubman, Conductor of the Underground Railroad
by Kate McMullan, illustrated by Steven James Petruccio

The Civil War

Lincoln: A Photobiography
by Russell Freedman

John Lincoln Clem: Civil War Drummer Boy
by E. F. Abbott, illustrated by Steven Noble

Seven Miles to Freedom: The Robert Smalls Story
by Janet Halfmann, illustrated by Duane Smith

Ancestral Puebloan cliff dwellings at Mesa Verde National Park in Colorado

The Indigenous Peoples of North America and First Encounters

For thousands of years, a wide variety of nations, tribes, and people groups moved throughout the continent, establishing villages, cities, governments, religious practices, agricultural systems, and all the various elements of civilization. Sometimes these nations went to war, empires rose and fell, people groups flourished, and some disappeared. Just as countries grew and faltered in ancient and medieval Europe, Asia, and Africa, the same pattern of history was working itself out in North America.

The Native Peoples of North America were responsible for remarkable achievements in architecture, transport, medicine, agriculture, and government. The most advanced architectural structures north of Mexico were the Cahokia Mounds. One of the great cities of the world, Cahokia was larger than London in 1250 AD. The Mississippians who lived here were accomplished builders who erected monumental public works that maintained their grandeur for centuries. Monks Mound, which took 300 years to build, towers 100 feet tall and is as wide as the Great Pyramid of Giza at its base.

introduction continued ...

The California Ohlone used advanced agricultural practices like controlled burns to clear dense underbrush, reducing the risk of wildfires and increasing crop yields. For hundreds of years, Iroquois and Wampanoag increased crop yields by planting multiple crops closely together in a practice known as intercropping, based on how various plants complement one another, improving health and growth. The Three Sisters—corn, beans, and squash—would be planted closely together, the corn providing the structure upon which the squash and beans could grow. Native Peoples first cultivated tobacco 1,000 years before Europeans arrived.

Native Peoples' vast knowledge of the healing and nutritional properties of roots and plants enabled them to effectively treat common sicknesses and viruses. Native Americans utilized more than 200 botanicals, which have been or are still in use in pharmaceuticals.

In transportation, birchbark canoes made by Algonquin and Ojibwa tribes were perfectly adapted to summer travel through the network of shallow streams, ponds, lakes, and swift rivers of the Northeast. Their lightness, easy maneuverability, and beauty are still prized today. The California Chumash's remarkable canoe-making skills enabled them to travel great distances out to sea to pursue large fish such as swordfish. The canoes were fashioned from redwood that drifted to shore from northern forests which, when pitched with tar, could carry up to twenty men. Native Peoples invented snowshoes and ice fishing and were the first to make maple syrup.

Natives also developed sophisticated methods of governance. The Iroquois Confederacy was so inspiring to the founding fathers that aspects of it were incorporated into the Articles of Confederation and U.S. Constitution. Indeed, in 1751 Benjamin Franklin described the need for the thirteen colonies to form a "voluntary Union" similar to that of the Iroquois Confederacy. We will learn more about this in the book *Hiawatha and the Peacemaker* by Robbie Robertson.

While much of the history of the Americas has been lost or blotted out through conquest, the work of historians, anthropologists, archaeologists, and Native storytellers continually adds to our knowledge. One of the challenges in learning about these various cultures comes from language barriers and a lack of written records. Most Indigenous American peoples had a strong and robust tradition of oral storytelling. These oral histories were passed down from generation to generation and, as cultures disappeared, merged, or were conquered, some of these stories and records disappeared. But not all was lost.

Today there is a renaissance in Native storytelling. Native scholars and historians track down these histories, stories, and legends, giving us a greater knowledge of the past. In this section, we will learn about a few of the nations or tribes that flourished in North America before Europeans arrived. These provide just a small sampling of the Indigenous Peoples. As you learn more about the Mohawk, Longhouse, Wampanoag, Seneca, and others, do some research on the tribes that lived in your area. There are probably local museums dedicated to preserving the cultures and traditions they have passed down to their descendants. See if you can learn more about your local tribes at powwows.com. We also encourage you to use the Rabbit Trails to explore further.

We will be reading about the Wampanoag, Iroquois, and Mohawk in this section, as well as the first Europeans to make their way across the Atlantic over 1,000 years ago.

Rabbit Trails

Where the Buffaloes Begin
by Olaf Baker and illustrated by Stephen Gammell
Olaf Baker's first-person account of life among the Blackfoot captures the strength, resilience, and independence of this Indigenous tribe.

We Asked for Nothing: The Remarkable Journey of Cabeza de Vaca
by Stuart Waldman
In 1528 the conquistador Alvar Núñez Cabeza de Vaca was shipwrecked on Texas's coast and rescued by Karankawa Indians. For eight years he shared life with various Southwestern tribes and survived because of them. Returning to Spain, De Vaca became an advocate for the New World's Indigenous people. Highly recommended.

Gift Horse: A Lakota Story by S. D. Nelson
As a member of the Standing Rock Sioux Tribe, Nelson drew inspiration for this story from his great-great-grandfather. Young Flying Cloud and his horse Storm go through tests of stamina, courage, and faithfulness.

Turtle Island: The Story of North America's First People
by Eldon Yellowhorn and Kathy Lowinger &
The Girl Who Helped Thunder: And Other Native American Folktales
by Joseph Bruchac
Both anthologies present traditional folktales and myths of America's Indigenous people teaching humility, respect, and gratitude.

Before Columbus: The Americas of 1491 by Charles C. Mann
Building from archeological artifacts and DNA evidence, the story of Indigenous Peoples in the Americas becomes ever more complex and fascinating. From genetic engineering of maize to remarkable structures like the Cahokia Mounds, America's first inhabitants' stories make up a valuable part of our American heritage.

Indians written and illustrated by Edwin Tunis
Mr. Tunis has re-created here, in spectacular detail, every meaningful aspect of a past way of life. The author's devotion to honoring and recording the customs, arts, and traditions in 245 accurate drawings is a treasure store that continues to speak over sixty years after its original publication.

Character Connection: imago Dei

Imago Dei is a foundational Christian idea stretching back to the earliest writings of Judaism, the historical and theological ancestor of Christianity. Genesis 1:27 reads:

> So God created mankind
> in his own image,
> in the image of God
> he created them;
> male and female
> he created them.

This passage is the foundation for the idea that all people bear God's image, or imago Dei. This idea is the foundation for a Christian understanding of human worth and dignity. Since every human being is an image-bearer of God, every life is precious, and every person is inherently valuable and worthy. Sadly, because we live in a fallen world and evil is very present and real, the imago Dei is often violated and ignored. We will read stories that bear witness to the suffering that comes when imago Dei is violated, as well as learn about heroic individuals who risked everything to stand up for human dignity. We will see the world-changing power of defending the imago Dei in all people.

As you read the literature in this section, look for examples of when the imago Dei is respected and when it is violated. What are the outcomes? How does reverence for imago Dei lead to better relationships and a better world? When is it difficult for the characters in the story to live by the idea of imago Dei even though they may not believe in this specific principle?

Crafts & Projects

Build a Model Native Home

Instructions to build a very simple model longhouse: https://classroom.synonym.com/make-longhouse-school-project-5836407.html

Video from the Homeschool Scene YouTube channel, "Homeschool with me: DIY Longhouse"

Search online for instructions on how to make an Iroquois longhouse.

Wampum Activities

Explore symbols and design of wampum belts with this craft from the American Revolution Museum: www.amrevmuseum.org/make-your-own-wampum-belt-craft

Create a virtual wampum belt: www.nativetech.org/beadwork/wampumgraph/index.html

Native American Diorama

Instruct your student to research a Native tribe and build a shoebox diorama incorporating the following elements: traditional housing, food, dress, and other distinguishing features.

Find inspiration at the following sites:

http://mrscoxhces.blogspot.com/2013/01/native-american-dioramas.html

http://theartoflearning-bermingham.blogspot.com/2014/12/project-annual-native-american-dioramas.html

Make a Talking Stick

Learn about talking sticks and follow the instructions to create your own: http://homeschoolfridays.com/make-your-own-talking-stick/

Draw a Viking Ship

Introduction to drawing a simple Viking longboat: https://drawinglessonsfortheyoungartist.blogspot.com/2011/11/how-to-draw-viking-ship-lesson-for.html

An inspiring blog post for creating gorgeous 3D Viking ship paintings: https://cassiestephens.blogspot.com/2013/11/in-artroom-4th-grade-viking-ships.html

Create a Viking ship collage: https://cassiestephens.blogspot.com/2013/10/in-art-room-viking-ship-collages.html

Build a Viking Longboat

"DIY: Viking Longship" on Wesprout YouTube channel

Simple print-and-paste template for building a basic Viking longboat using paper, cardboard, and glue: www.crayola.com/free-coloring-pages/print/viking-ship-coloring-page/

Free download of printable Viking longboat model: www.forbicolla.it/res/site118454/res771747_pagina-A4-gratis-5.jpg

Dress Up Like a Viking

A very simple Viking costume reference sheet: https://vikingschoolvisits.com/wp-content/uploads/2018/12/Viking-day-dressing-up-sheet.pdf

Make a Viking Shield

This website provides instructions to make wood and metal Viking shields in various degrees of difficulty. These are definitely advanced. https://sonsofvikings.com/blogs/vikings-tv-series/how-to-make-your-own-viking-shield

A very basic and simple Viking shield project: www.hobbycraft.co.uk/ideas/kids/how-to-make-a-viking-shield

Upcycled Viking craft project using common household items: https://deceptivelyeducational.blogspot.com/2013/01/viking-shield-upcycled-history-craft.html

Rabbit Trails: Vikings

The D'Aulaires Book of Norse Myths
by Ingri and Edgar Parin d'Aulaire
This classic will enrich your study by introducing the colorful characters of Norse mythology. Students will delight in getting to know Thor the thunder god, Odin the All-father, Loki (the Jotun's mischievous god), the beautiful Freya, and the kind and just Balder, who is so full of light that he simply cannot be unhappy.

Hakon of Rogen's Saga by Erik Christian Haugaard
The author delved into several volumes of the Icelandic sagas to understand the background of the story he wanted to write, but it was camping in the Norwegian fjords that brought true inspiration. In the tale, we meet Hakon, whose mother dies giving birth to him and whose tragic childhood gives him wisdom beyond his years. Seeking to claim his birthright, Hakon must confront the violence and deceit so rife in the Viking era.

Sword Song by Rosemary Sutcliff
The young Norseman Bjarni Sigurdson is just 16 when he is charged with manslaying and banished from his Northern Ireland settlement. For five years, he makes his way alone in the world, selling his sword-service (fighting ability) to willing chieftains who make their fortunes by pillaging and raiding villages in the scattered isles of the North Sea.

Across a Dark and Wild Sea by Don Brown
In the year 521 in Ireland, a young boy named Columcille was born into a princely tribe but forsook his pagan heritage to join the church and devote his life to learning. He was so enamored with a borrowed book of Psalms that he painstakingly copied it out in secret. When the owner discovered the copy, he demanded it. Columcille's refusal resulted in a battle, which cost 3,000 lives.

Barbarians! by Steven Kroll and illustrated by Robert Byrd
Goths, Huns, Vikings, and Mongols are featured here in an engaging text with delightfully detailed illustrations.

Beowulf

Any study of the Vikings would hardly be complete without an introduction to the most famous epic of the Viking era—*Beowulf*. Considered the first epic in English, Beowulf's adventures follow the hero's journey as he seeks to rescue the Danes from the monster Grendel's ravages. Look for the editions featured above by the following authors: Nicky Raven, Michael Morpurgo, James Rumford, Gareth Hinds, and Kevin Crossley-Holland. The illustrations in the Morpurgo edition are exquisite, but if you have a sensitive student, perhaps use either the Rumford or the Crossley-Holland edition. Fans of graphic novels will enjoy Gareth Hind's work. As the epic contains violence, please preview any edition beforehand.

Ball-play of the Choctaw by George Catlin, c. 1846–1850

LESSON 1

1. Introduce *A Child's First Book of American History* by Earl Schenck Miers, hereafter referred to as *A Child's First*. Read "A Call to Adventure" on pages 8-9.

a. On page 9, Miers presents a list of ideals commonly held by citizens of the United States. Define *ideals* and discuss why it is important for a nation to have them. Are there any you would add to Miers's list? How do you think our country has lived up to those ideals?

b. What do you think the author meant when he wrote that the U.S. "now stands at its most challenging moment"? What challenges do you believe our nation faces?

c. It has been said that the purpose of studying history is to "instruct and inform." How can learning about the past be helpful for the present moment? Discuss these ideas in light of the following quotes:

"The past is always a rebuke to the present." Robert Penn Warren
"A country without a memory is a country of madmen." George Santayana
"History teaches everything including the future." Lamartine
"We are not makers of history. We are made by history." Martin Luther King Jr.

2. Teach your student "The Continents" song. Watch "Seven Continents" on the Rachel Coleman YouTube channel.

3. Have your student cut out the world map from the Picture Packet and paste it into the notebook. Have your student color and label each continent.

LESSON 2

1. Have your student begin a new section in the notebook titled "The Indigenous Peoples of North America" and cut out the Early Localization of Native Tribes map from the Picture Packet and paste it into the notebook. This map documents what we know about the locations of Native tribes and nations just before European arrival.

2. We will now begin reading about the Wampanoag. Locate their lands on the map in the notebook near Cape Cod, Massachusetts. Study the other areas of the map and see if you can recognize familiar tribes. Introduce *People of the Breaking Day* by Marcia Sewall and study the cover artwork. Read pages 5-15.

a. Why do the Wampanoag call themselves "People of the Breaking Day"? What do they call the sun and how do they greet it? *The Wampanoag live on the coastline of Massachusetts where they can see the sun's first beams as it rises each morning. The Wampanoag greet the Nippa'uus, or sun, by thanking it for its "warmth and light and beauty."*

b. What do the Wampanoag call God? *Kiehtan, which translates as "the Great Spirit."*

c. Are the Wampanoag hunter-gatherers? *The Wampanoag hunt and gather, but they are not solely hunter-gatherers since they also cultivate crops.*

d. What is the Neepunnakee'wush moon, and how is it celebrated? *The Neepunnakee'wush moon is the harvest moon, marked by a week of feasting, dancing, games, and song.*

e. Who was the great sachem of the Wampanoag? What were his duties? *Massasoit was the great sachem, and he was responsible for finding the best hunting, fishing, and farming areas; he meted out discipline for lawbreakers and decided when to go to war.*

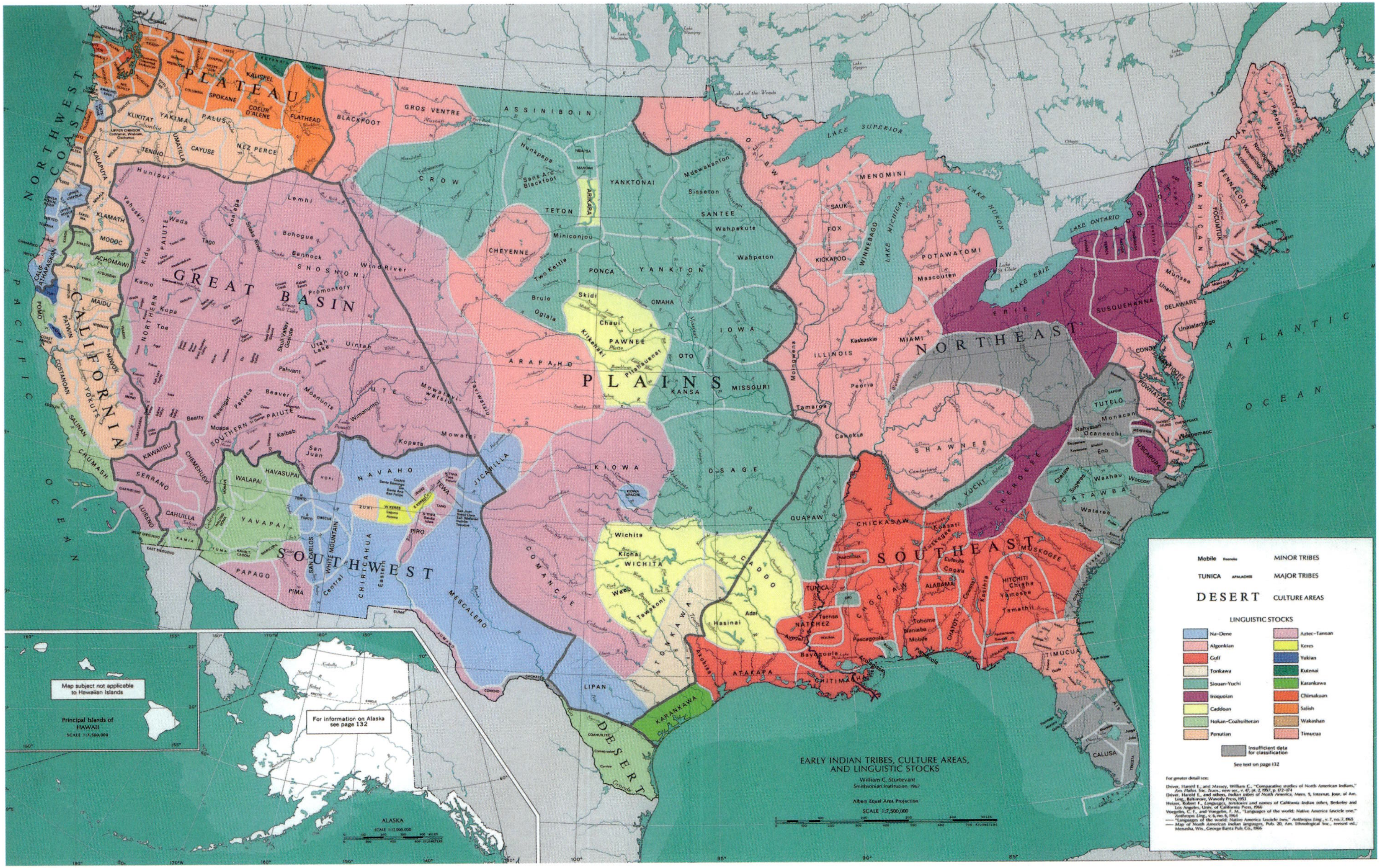

Early Localization of Native Americans

LESSON 3

1. Read pages 16-32 of *People of the Breaking Day.*

a. What are some of the responsibilities of the father of the family? How are these similar or different from modern-day fathers? *The Wampanoag father had similar duties to modern fathers. He selected the best habitation for his family, provided food, set up the wetu framework, and provided transportation by making a dugout canoe for fishing and trading. Wampanoag fathers are different from modern fathers in that they must study nature, watch the seasons, know the plants and animals upon which their lives depend, and be proficient at all the skills necessary to hunt, fish, and trap.*

b. Who does the farming in the Wampanoag family? What crop do the men insist on growing themselves? *The women are the tribe's farmers, but the men insist on growing the ottomma'ocke–tobacco.*

c. Why do Wampanoag families keep their babies' names secret? *In the Wampanoag belief system, names are sacred. If names are used openly, they lose their power.*

d. What role do the children play in providing for their families? *Wampanoag children help with fetching water, gathering firewood, digging clams, helping plant crops, shooing birds away from newly planted fields, and tending the fires that smoked fish, clams, eel, and meats like venison and turkey.*

e. How do the Wampanoags fertilize their crops? *The women place a herring or chopped-up horseshoe crabs in the soil to fertilize it.*

f. How do the Wampanoag know that winter is near? *When the locusts begin to sing, the Wampanoag know that winter is near.*

2. The Eastern chipmunk was, and continues to be, widespread in the areas settled by the Wampanoag. Cut out the Eastern chipmunk image from the Picture Packet and have your student color and add it to the notebook along with a few facts from your research.

LESSON 4

1. Read pages 33-45 of *People of the Breaking Day.*

a. Why do the Wampanoag men hunt deer in the fall? *Deer are hunted in the fall because they are the fattest at that time.*

b. Before winter sets in, where do the Wampanoag go? *The Wampanoag move inland, away from the sea with its cold winds and storms.*

c. How are young Wampanoag boys prepared for manhood? *Wampanoag boys must spend a winter alone in the deep forest and learn how to survive there.*

2. To conclude your study of the Wampanoag, have the student write and illustrate a brief report on the Wampanoag. If desired, have your student copy some of the Wampanoag words from *People of the Breaking Day* into the glossary.

The Vikings

Around 1000 AD, Nordic Vikings touched on a continent entirely unknown to the Europeans. They encountered Native people there who likewise knew nothing of the vast continents that lay across the waters to the east. In the course of our study, we will learn about both of these worlds, the people who inhabited them, and how the meeting of two worlds would set off a chain of events and encounters that would change human history forever. We begin with the Vikings, as their landing in North America was the first link in that chain. Of course, they didn't know that they had happened upon an entire continent, but their legends of that first landing would travel through history, inspiring the journey of other curious explorers—namely, one Christopher Columbus.

Historical records confirm that these Nordic peoples were brutal conquerors. Running out of land and space in their native northern lands, the Vikings began raiding Europe in 793 AD in search of both new lands and treasure. Their pagan beliefs meant that they felt no qualms about attacking unarmed churches and monasteries. Of course, this callousness to the divine made the Vikings even more fearsome to the religious Europeans! Over time these raids turned to trade as Vikings settled throughout Europe, setting up trading posts that would eventually become famous cities like Dublin.

One Viking clan had discovery and conquest running deep in its veins. Eric the Red was the great-great-grandnephew of Iceland's discoverer, and he would go on to discover Greenland. His son, Leif, would lead that first expedition to the land that would come to be known as North America. Their story is one of conquest but also conversion and changing values.

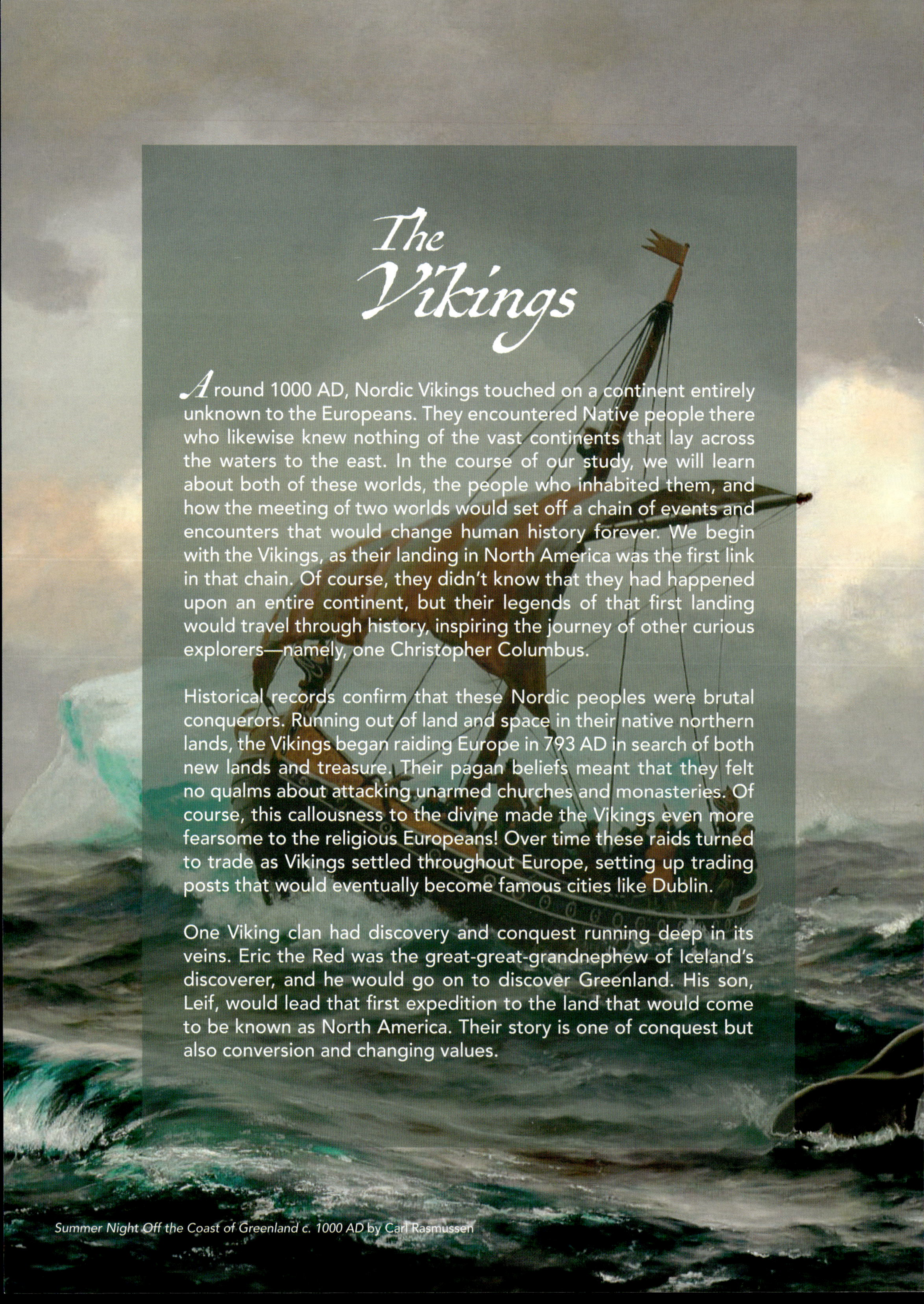

Summer Night Off the Coast of Greenland c. 1000 AD by Carl Rasmussen

LESSON 5

1. The Wampanoag were but one of thousands of tribes and First Nations who had lived on the continent for thousands of years before Europeans landed on America's eastern shores. The first recorded encounter between Natives and Europeans happened around 1000 AD. We will now turn our attention to this brief but historically significant time. Familiarity with the following Nordic and nautical terms is recommended. In preparation for this section, have your student define the following terms and record them in the glossary of their student notebook:

prow	promontory	thrall
rune	fiord	saga
coracle	rigging	bearings (nautical)
headland	inlet	flotilla
shoal	men-at-arms	berserker
venison	relic	marooned
keel		

2. Introduce *The Vikings* by Elizabeth Janeway. Read the Foreword and Chapter 1. As you read through this book, it will be helpful to refer to the photographs of Viking artifacts beginning on page 135.

a. What was Brendan's relationship with Leif? Where was Brendan from? *Brendan was a thrall, essentially a slave, to Leif. He was captured during a Viking raid in Ireland.*

b. Why was Eric banished from Haukadal? *Eric avenged the murder of his thralls by killing Eyulf, a free man. The penalty levied for killing a free man was banishment from the region.*

3. Have your student begin a new section in the notebook and title it "The Vikings." From the Picture Packet, have your student cut out the map of the north Atlantic region and label England, Ireland, Iceland, Greenland, and Nova Scotia. Have your student color and paste it into the notebook.

4. To learn more about St. Brendan, watch "Voyage of St. Brendan" on the fundermation YouTube channel.

LESSON 6

1. Read Chapter 2 of *The Vikings.*

a. Was Eric able to control his anger when he heard Thorgest had taken his homestead? Why did Eric return to Haukadal? What was the result of his decision? *No, Eric was outraged. Eric returned to Haukadal to take back his property by force. Eric and his followers killed six men and lost two of their own.*

b. It is mentioned in this chapter that Brendan and Leif play checkers. This is a bit inaccurate as the game they were likely playing was Hnefatafl, a precursor to checkers widely played by Scandinavians and Celts in the medieval period. A small but passionate group of people still play this ancient game.

2. Visit the following website to learn more about the Viking thrall, or slavery, system:
https://en.natmus.dk/historical-knowledge/denmark/prehistoric-period-until-1050-ad/the-viking-age/power-and-aristocracy/slaves-and-thralls/

3. Have your student write out the Viking rune alphabet in the notebook. The following website has some fun activities to teach your student more about runes, including decoding secret rune messages:
www.teachingideas.co.uk/vikings/the-viking-alphabet

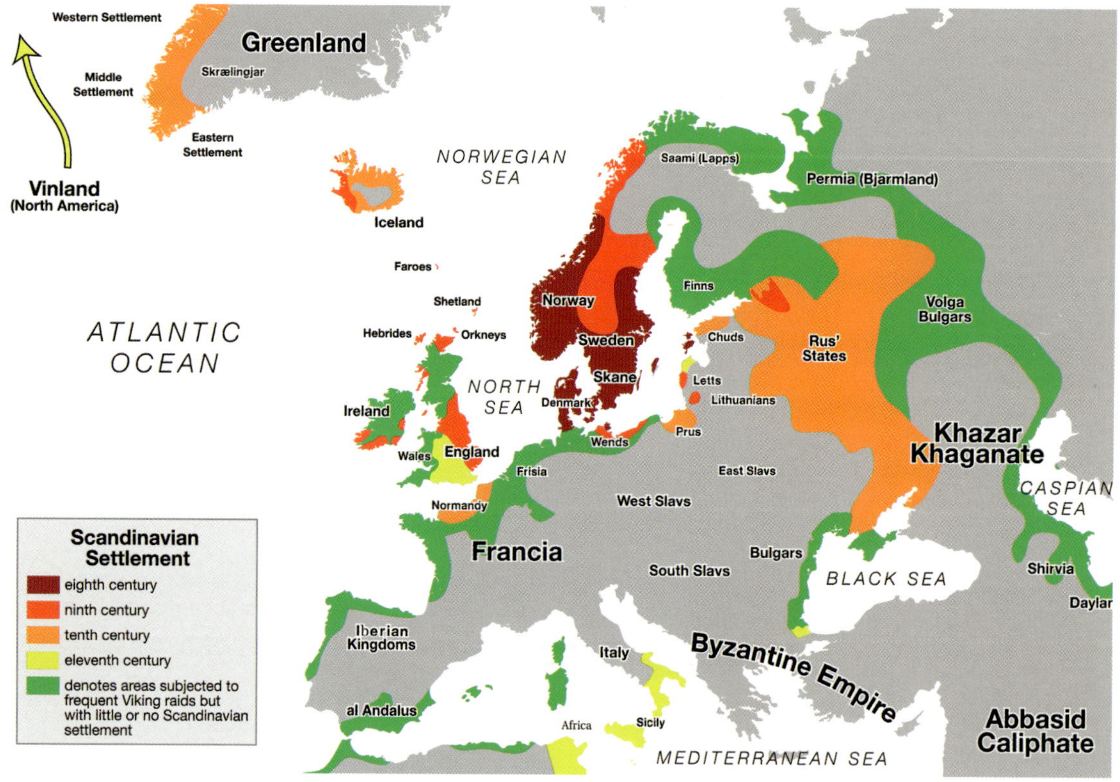

1. Detail of the runic inscription found on one of the copies of the golden horns of Gallehus, c. 400 AD.
2. Codex Runicus, c. 1300. 3. Scandinavian settlement between 700-1000 AD.

LESSON 7

1. Read Chapter 3 of *The Vikings.*

    a. What did the men find that Brendan claimed were made by the first Irish settlers? *They found a skin boat made of animal hide and whale bones. They also found ivory and bone needles, a comb, and a stone ax.*

    b. How long did the Vikings stay in Greenland? *Three years.*

2. Viking ships had a long and proud history stretching long before the time of Eric the Red! Do some research on the history of longships and have your student record findings in the notebook. Watch "What's so special about Viking Ships?" on the TedEd YouTube channel.

3. From Crafts and Projects on page 10, choose one of the Draw a Viking Ship activities and have your student work on it. When completed, add to the notebook.

LESSON 8

1. Read Chapter 4 of *The Vikings.*

    a. How many ships set sail for Greenland? How many made the journey successfully? *25 ships set sail for Greenland, but only 14 ships safely made the voyage.*

    b. What did Bjarni promise Leif? *Bjarni told Leif that he could borrow his ship to sail further west to the lands beyond Greenland.*

2. To learn more about how the Vikings lived, watch the following video: "Vikings for Kids // History for Kids" on The Touring Teacher YouTube channel.

3. Have your student choose a Viking craft or project from page 10.

LESSON 9

1. Read Chapter 5 of *The Vikings.*

    a. What skills did Thorhall teach Leif and Brendan? *Thorhall taught them how to hunt with a bow and arrows, with spears, and by setting traps. They also learned how to collect the down of Eider ducks and capture Greenland falcons.*

    b. How did Eric respond when Leif asked for a ship? *Eric initially called Leif a child but then realized that his son had grown into a man. Eric told Leif he may use his ship if he sailed east to Norway before adventuring westward.*

    c. Was it wise for Leif to hire a pilot to navigate the Norwegian coast? *Yes. The Norwegian coast is dangerous, and it was wise to have an experienced pilot navigate it.*

    d. Why did Brendan believe the king would like their gifts? *Brendan knew that their unique gifts from Greenland would stand out to the king, who was used to receiving gold and jewels.*

    e. Where does our common phrase "going berserk" come from? *"Going berserk" is derived from berserker warriors who could drive themselves into a fury before battle. They would work themselves up so much that in battle they would hardly feel a wound.*

LESSON 10

1. Read Chapter 6 of *The Vikings.*

 a. How did Leif defeat Ketil? Did Leif display good sportsmanship in the duel? *Leif outsmarted Ketil and exploited Ketil's furious anger to his advantage. Leif insisted that Ketil's wounds were cared for and wrapped to prevent him from dying.*

2. Have your student choose a Viking craft or project from page 10.

LESSON 11

1. Read Chapter 7 of *The Vikings.*

 a. What did Olaf tell Leif to consider? Did Leif become a Christian? *The king asked Leif to consider Christianity, and Leif was baptized.*

 b. Who did Eric demand Leif take with him on his voyage west? *The German Tyrker.*

2. Vikings are often depicted as wearing helmets with fearsome horns jutting out on either side. Have your student do some research on the accuracy of this portrayal. Where did this idea come from? Is there evidence that Vikings wore horned helmets? Have your student record findings in the notebook.

LESSON 12

1. Read Chapter 8 of *The Vikings.*

 a. How did the landscape change as they went south? *The first land they saw was barren, flat, and covered in large stones, while further south, it was well-treed. Still further south, the land featured bays, lakes, rivers, sandy beaches, larger trees, bountiful game, and fish.*

 b. Did Leif achieve what he set out to do? *Leif achieved his goal of finding the land Bjarni had seen.*

2. Using the description of Leif's voyage on page 93 of *The Vikings*, have your student chart this historic voyage on a globe or map. Have your student mark the journey on the map in the notebook. The following websites will be helpful:

 https://www.pinterest.com/pin/341640321733586070/
 www.webexhibits.org/vinland/archeological.html

LESSON 13

1. Read Chapter 9 of *The Vikings.*

 a. How did Leif demonstrate good leadership? *Leif was diligent in building a shelter that could be defended against possible enemies. He was careful in exploring the land with a strong force with the Irish runners scouting ahead. He also had his men fish, set traps, and store up provisions for the winter.*

 b. Who did Leif happen upon on his return voyage to Greenland? *They happened upon a shipwrecked Norwegian ship. They rescued the crew and brought them to Brattahlid.*

2. While the Vikings would have been familiar with polar bears, they may have been surprised to see black bears in Newfoundland. Cut out the black bear image from the Picture Packet and have your student color and add it to the notebook along with a few facts from your research.

3. Have your student cut out, color, and paste the Leif Erikson picture on the timeline.

LESSON 14

1. Read Chapter 10 of *The Vikings.*

   a. Why did Leif decide to stay in Greenland and not return to Vineland? *Now that Eric was dead, Brattahlid was Leif's responsibility, and he had to care for his mother and the people who were loyal to him. He could not sail to Vineland and start a new life, for Eric had left all he had to Leif.*

   b. Discuss the Vikings' first encounter with the Native people in Vineland. Imagine this experience from both the Viking and the Native perspectives. What would it be like to meet people who looked, dressed, spoke, and acted entirely different from you? Given that the Natives were unarmed, how could Thorvald and his men have responded differently? How was the Viking response typical of their culture of conquest?

   c. How did Karlsefni respond to Leif's stories about Vineland? *Karlsefni felt that Vineland was a place to not only explore but also settle permanently.*

2. Have your student begin working on a one-page written report, picture collage, or oral presentation on Leif Erikson's life. One fun way is to dress up as Leif and present his life story in a dramatic performance. Choose whatever format you would most enjoy. Include the approximate date and place of Leif's birth, information on his parents, his voyage to Norway and Christian conversion, and his discoveries.

3. In the 1960s, archaeologists working in Newfoundland discovered evidence of a Viking colony dating back to 1000. Read all about it at the following links:
   www.newfoundlandlabrador.com/destinations/lanse-aux-meadows
   www.nationalgeographic.com/travel/canada/l-anse-aux-meadows-newfoundland/

LESSON 15

1. Conclude *The Vikings* by reading Chapter 11 and the Afterword. Note: This chapter includes unflattering references to the Native peoples as recorded by the Vikings in their chronicles. These descriptions present an opportunity to discuss how strangers perceive one another, how differences can appear threatening, and how dissimilar groups can vilify one another. We have seen that the Vikings were wild and fierce. If we met a Viking today, we would hardly consider him civilized. The Natives probably thought the same of these pale, light-haired invaders, just like the Vikings believed the Natives were wild and threatening. When reading this account of the Vikings and the Natives' meetings, keep in mind what the Natives could have been thinking. We do not have a record of their side of the story, so it requires some imagination to put ourselves in their shoes.

   a. What happened to Thorhall? *Thorhall disagreed with Karlsefni's plan to sail south in search of suitable land, so Karlsefni gave Thorhall and his men a small boat to sail north. They ran into a terrible storm that blew them across the Atlantic to Ireland, where they were enslaved. Brendan heard about this and bought Thorhall out of slavery. The difficulty of the Atlantic voyage weakened Thorhall, and he did not live much longer.*

   b. What did Karlsefni learn from the story of the Viking's first bloody encounter with the Natives? How did he approach establishing relationships with the "Skraeling" differently from Thorvald? Were the Vikings and Natives able to establish peaceful relationships? *Karlsefni stated, "We will have no fighting if we can help it!" Karlsefni's diplomacy led the way to two peaceful encounters with the Natives. While we have no record of how the Natives felt about these invaders establishing a settlement on their land, the continuing conflict discouraged Karlsefni. He returned to Greenland with his company.*

2. Read Chapter 1 of *A Child's First.*

3. Conclude this section of our study with a reading of your student's report or presentation on the life of Leif Erikson. This could take place during a Viking feast! Dress up as Vikings, prepare the recipes found in The Historic Table on pages 28-31, and discuss what you learned and your favorite things about the Vikings! You could even play some Viking music (www.viking.no/e/life/music/).

Iroquois: Five Nations c.1142

1. Iroquois Nations, c. 1142.
2. Iroquois painting of Tadodaho receiving two Mohawk chiefs.

LESSON 16

1. Our next book tells the story of how the Five Nations Iroquois Confederacy came to be. Like most founding stories, it combines history with legend, religion, and fantasy. Locate the Iroquois Confederacy near Lake Ontario on the map in your student's notebook. Introduce *Hiawatha and the Peacemaker* by Robbie Robertson and David Shannon. Read the first third of the book through the page that ends with the sentence: "Together we paddled as one nation."

    a. Have your student narrate Hiawatha's story to this point.

    b. How did Hiawatha spend his days after his wife and daughters were killed? Discuss his emotions. How does the human instinct for revenge lead to feuding and war? *Hiawatha wanders around in a fog consumed by anger, hunger, sleeplessness, and thoughts of revenge. The need to avenge wrong is never satisfied and creates more pain and tragedy.*

    c. Throughout this book, you will encounter symbolism. For example, the Peacemaker arrived on a morning when the mist had burned off the river. His arrival was accompanied by light. This image helps the reader see that the Peacemaker brought a change to the darkness in Hiawatha's mind and life.

    d. What is the Great Law? *"Peace, power, and righteousness shall be the new way. All nations will become one family. Our people shall have one body, one mind, and one heart."*

LESSON 17

1. The Peacemaker gave Hiawatha a string of wampum shells when they met. Research the purpose of wampum and have your student record key points in the notebook. Learn more by watching the video at the following link: Marcus Hendricks from the Wampanoag preserves traditional methods for creating wampum beads and belts: www.pbs.org/video/traditional-wampum-belts-gy05in/

2. Watch "North America's Ancient Cities" at history.com to learn more about pre-encounter Native American history: www.history.com/videos/north-americas-ancient-cities

3. Read the middle section of *Hiawatha and the Peacemaker*, up through the page that ends with the sentence: "Together we paddled as four nations."

    a. Have your student narrate Hiawatha's story to this point.

    b. What word freed Hiawatha from the anger and sadness he had felt since Tadodaho killed his family? *Forgiveness.*

    c. What did the Clan Mother mean when she scolded the Mohawk people, "You reject Tadodaho, but you behave just like him!" *The Clan Mother referred to their "closed ears and closed minds" and the habit of resorting to violence to solve their differences.*

4. Have your student choose an activity from the Crafts and Projects section on page 10.

LESSON 18

1. Finish reading *Hiawatha and the Peacemaker*, including the Historical Note and Author's Note.

  a. How has the evil in Tadodaho's heart transformed him into a monster? *Tadodaho lived apart from his people, and his body was twisted and hunched over. Scales covered his body, and snakes sprouted from his head. He had lost the ability to speak and only made hissing sounds.*

  b. Did Tadodaho immediately join the other nations? What did Hiawatha and the Peacemaker do to change Tadodaho's heart? *They showed him a better way, both through the beauty of their song and the kindness of their actions. Hiawatha served Tadodaho and offered him forgiveness as well as peace, power, and righteousness.*

  c. What honor was bestowed upon Tadodaho? *He became the keeper of the peace.*

2. The Five Nations formed the oldest ongoing participatory democracy on earth! The date of the founding is unknown, but scholars have determined that it may have happened as early as 1142 AD. The Five Nation's commitment to equality was unparalleled at the time, causing one British administrator to say that the Iroquois had "such absolute Notions of Liberty that they allow no Kind of Superiority of one over another, and banish all Servitude from their Territories." Have your student record a brief history of the story behind this coalition in the notebook along with its influence on the formation of the United States after consulting the following resources:
www.pbs.org/native-america/blogs/native-voices/how-the-iroquois-great-law-of-peace-shaped-us-democracy/
www.senate.gov/reference/resources/pdf/hconres331.pdf

3. Have your student cut out, color, and paste the Iroquois Confederacy picture on the timeline.

LESSON 19

1. Introduce *Children of the Longhouse* by Joseph Bruchac, a Nulhegan Abenaki citizen and elder. Using oral tradition and research, he writes stories that truly bring to life the customs, practices, and cultures of North American Indigenous Peoples. This story takes place around 1400 in the Iroquois, or Haudenosaunee, Nation. Study the map and diagram that appear after the inscription in *Children of the Longhouse*. Read Chapters 1-2.

  a. How did Grabber reduce the humanity of the Anen:taks? *He said, "Those eaters of bark are not real men. They are cowards."*

  b. Why was Grabber's plan so dangerous? *It threatened the peace between the Flint Nation, or Mohawks, and the Anen:taks, placing everyone in danger.*

  c. What do you think about Ohkwa'ri telling his grandmother what he heard? When She Opens the Sky asked Ohkwa'ri if he would tell the story in front of Grabber and his friends, how did Ohkwa'ri respond? What does this tell us about Ohkwa'ri? *Ohkwa'ri said that he would repeat Grabber's words in front of him at the ceremony. This bold statement shows that Ohkwa'ri cared more about his people's welfare than about his safety. He was courageous.*

  d. What are the Three Sisters? *The staples of the Iroquois diet: squash, corn, and beans.*

2. Ohkwa'ri, a Mohawk, lived in a longhouse. Print out the PDF available at the following site to learn more about traditional Native houses. Have your student cut out and label the illustrations and add them to the notebook. montessoriforeveryone.com/assets/free_downloads/Native_American_Homes.pdf

3. Using the diagram titled "The Great League of Peace" at the beginning of *Children of the Longhouse* as a guide, have your student draw their own diagram illustrating the relationships between the nations of the Great League of Peace and the villages and clans of the Mohawk. Add the diagram to the notebook.

LESSON 20

1. *Children of the Longhouse* introduced us to a few of the Mohawk peoples' principles and ideals. These are seen in the qualities that the Clan Mothers seek in the leaders they choose. What are those qualities, and what do they tell us about the values of the Mohawk? If needed, review pages 22-23 of *Children of the Longhouse.* Learn more about the Clan Mothers and their responsibilities here: www.onondaganation.org/government/clan-mothers/

2. Read Chapters 3-4 of *Children of the Longhouse.*

   a. Describe the relationship between the Mohawk and the Anen:taks before their treaty. Why was it so crucial that Grabber's plan be stopped? *When the Mohawk came to the Anen:tak's land and tried to settle there, the Anen:tak drove them out or captured and enslaved them. The Mohawk and Anen:tak eventually made peace and began to trade with one another. Grabber's plan put the peace in peril, risking death and enslavement.*

3. Big Tree told the story of the Mohawk ancestors' migration. It seems to indicate that they came from the Mississippi and Missouri Rivers region. This would make it possible that the Mohawk were descendants of peoples known collectively as the Mound Builders. Have your student research Cahokia, the largest city built by the Mound Builders, and record key points in the notebook.

4. Ohkwa'ri finds an Eastern cottontail rabbit nest in Chapter 4. Cut out the Eastern cottontail rabbit image from the Picture Packet, and have your student color and add it to the notebook along with a few facts from your research.

LESSON 21

1. Read Chapters 5-6 of *Children of the Longhouse.*

   a. Otsi:stia recalled her people's creation story. What were the original teachings of the Creator? *Human beings should be kind to each other, be thankful, and show respect for all things.*

   b. In our readings of *Children of the Longhouse*, we have learned several of the legends, historical stories, and myths of the Mohawk people. These stories helped Ohkwa'ri and Otsi:stia learn many things, including their people's cultural values. Does your family have stories about where you came from? What do these family histories teach? Do you have a favorite?

2. Learn more about the Haudenosaunee people by watching "Haudenosaunee or Iroquois?" on the nysmuseum YouTube channel.

3. Herons Flying's name signifies the importance of this noble bird to the Mohawk people. Cut out the great blue heron image from the Picture Packet and have your student color and add to the notebook along with a few facts from your research.

1. Iroquois delegates to England: Tee Yee Neen Ho Ga Row, Ho Nee Yeath Taw No Row, Sa Ga Yeath Qua Pieth Tow, and Etow Oh Koam, painted by Jan Verelst, 1710. 2. *Ball Players* by George Catlin.

LESSON 22

1. Read Chapters 7-9 of *Children of the Longhouse.*

   a. Why was it considered improper to make much of a gift? *"The giver did not give the gift to be thanked for it but because the giving was from the heart."*

   b. Why do you think Thunder's Voice asked Ohkwa'ri to play in his place?

   c. Discuss the council meetings. How were matters debated? Was it essential that speakers wait for their turn? In general, in this story, were the characters quick to speak? Were they quick to offer their own opinions? Discuss the benefits and drawbacks of this intentional way of communicating.

2. Learn more about the history of Tekwaarathon, or lacrosse, at the following sites:

   Origin of lacrosse: www.history.com/news/lacrosse-origins-native-americans

   Choctaw Nation stickball history and game: "Ishtaboli: Little Brother of War" on the Choctaw Nation OK YouTube channel

   "Cherokee Nation Stickball" on the Cherokee Nation YouTube channel

3. The legend of Tekwaarathon references specific animals like the flying squirrel, the eagle, and the red-tailed hawk. Cut out the red-tailed hawk image from the Picture Packet, and have your student color and add it to the notebook along with a few facts from your research.

LESSON 23

1. Read Chapters 10-12 of *Children of the Longhouse.*

2. Have your student choose a Native American nation or tribe to research. You can have your student choose to create a diorama (see page 10), write a report, prepare an oral narration, or select another medium to communicate their findings. Work on this over the next 1-2 weeks.

LESSON 24

1. Finish reading *Children of the Longhouse*, including the Epilogue and Afterword.

   a. Have your student briefly narrate the story of Ohkwa'ri and Otsi:stia, focusing on his or her favorite parts.

2. If you have a *National Geographic* subscription or your library has access to the *National Geographic* archive, you can read Joseph Bruchac's original article on the Mohawk titled "A Mohawk Village in 1491." It appears in the October 1991 issue along with several excellent articles about other Native nations and tribes. **Note:** The illustrations do include historically accurate nudity.

3. Have your student finish working on their Native American research project.

Historic Table

Viking Lamb Stew or Sodd

Sodd is the Norwegian word "to seethe," and this Viking stew is an authentic reflection of a typical Viking meal. Because they were farmers, shepherds, and fishermen, they had access to abundant protein sources, but meat was generally served on special occasions. Potatoes were not introduced to Europe until the late-sixteenth century, so an authentic Viking stew would not include these but would have featured many other root vegetables.

2 pounds lamb stew meat trimmed of fat
2 lamb shanks
4 ounces butter (plus additional for frying)
1/4 cup bacon fat
1/3 cup all-purpose flour
5-6 garlic cloves, minced
1 large yellow onion, chopped
3 small leeks, chopped
3 shallots, chopped
1/2 celeriac (celery root), peeled and chopped
1 turnip, peeled and chopped
2-3 parsnips, chopped in rounds
3 carrots, chopped in rounds
3-4 potatoes, chopped (leave out for an authentic Viking dish)
3 tablespoons Madras curry powder
3 tablespoons sweet Hungarian paprika (or smoked paprika)
2 tablespoons whiskey (optional)
4-5 cups chicken bouillon
1 cup heavy cream (optional)
salt & freshly ground black pepper, to taste
lingonberry jam, as an accompaniment

Brown the butter with bacon fat in a Dutch oven or any heavy cast-iron pan. Add the curry powder and paprika and brown it until fragrant. Braise the meat a few pieces at a time until just browned, including the lamb shanks. Do not crowd; otherwise, the meat will steam and become tough. Just brown the meat; do not cook it. Set meat aside, and then to the same pan, add the chopped onion, leeks, garlic, and shallots. Stir to deglaze the pan. When the onion mixture is almost tender/clear, add the vegetables and sauté briefly. If you would prefer to add potatoes in the stew, add them about 15 minutes after the other vegetables to avoid overcooking. Add the flour, continually stirring to create a roux. Add the browned meat to the pan and just enough bouillon to cover the vegetables. Stir thoroughly. Add one tablespoon sea salt and a generous teaspoon of freshly ground pepper. Simmer on low until all the vegetables are tender—about an hour. Finally, stir in the optional whiskey and cream. Simmer briefly. Serve with hot crusty bread and lingonberry jam. This recipe is adapted from food.com.

VIKING 30

Historic Table

Viking Skyr Lingonberry Tarte

Skyr is Iceland's cross between Greek yogurt and cheese and is exceptionally high in protein and very creamy. The Vikings first created this superfood over 1,000 years ago using skim milk, enzymes, and fermentation. You can find it at Whole Foods and Walmart. The following recipe is adapted from siggis.com.

Shortbread Crust:

- 1 1/4 cups all-purpose flour
- 1/4 cup almond flour
- 1/2 cup powdered sugar
- 1/2 teaspoon salt
- 1 teaspoon vanilla
- 1 teaspoon grated lemon zest
- 1 1/2 sticks cold butter (6 ounces), cut into small pieces

Filling:

- 1 1/2 cups Skyr vanilla yogurt
- 1 teaspoon vanilla
- 1 packet gelatin
- 2 egg yolks
- 1/2 cup sugar or monk sugar
- 1/2 cup heavy whipping cream, whipped to peaks
- 1/3 cup lingonberry jam
- 1/4 cup raspberries or strawberries for garnish

Preheat oven to 350°F. Coat an 11" French tarte pan with non-stick cooking spray.

Mix shortbread ingredients until they resemble a coarse meal. Press crust mixture into the pie pan, forming an even layer on the bottom and sides. Prick lightly with a fork on the bottom. Bake in the oven for approximately 10-12 minutes, until lightly browned. Remove crust from oven and let cool.

While crust is cooling, whisk Skyr, egg yolks, vanilla, and sugar together. Place a tablespoon or two of water in a medium saucepan on the stove. Sprinkle the gelatin over it. When the gelatin begins to bloom, turn on the stove to a low heat. Add a little (a few tablespoons) of the Skyr mixture, whisking briskly over the low heat. Once it is mixed thoroughly, remove from heat and whisk in the whipped cream to the rest of the mixture. Pour into the cooled pie crust and refrigerate overnight. When the pie is set, garnish with lingonberry jam and raspberries or strawberries.

Historic Table

Three Sisters Stew

Indigenous Peoples made many dishes with the Three Sisters—corn, squash, and beans. The following is a modern adaptation that will be sure to please most young palates. I have adapted this recipe to be made with duck thighs and breasts, but any other stew meat—beef, lamb, or pork—will do. Duck can be found at Whole Foods seasonally and will lend a more authentic Native American flair. Try to use heritage beans, as these varieties have been preserved for generations by Indigenous People. Look for Tom's Mix at nativeseeds.org or check out the many varieties available at ramonafarms.com. Consider planting some native bean crops in a summer garden to honor the traditions and agricultural practices of Indigenous Peoples. Kabocha squash is generally available in the fall and is believed to have originated in the Americas. This recipe is adapted from the bonappetit.com site.

1-2 pounds duck thighs and breasts, or lamb, pork, or beef stew meat
2 teaspoons ground cumin
Kosher salt, as needed
Black pepper, as needed
1-2 tablespoons neutral oil, such as safflower
2 large yellow onions, diced
5 garlic cloves, minced
4 cups turkey or chicken stock, preferably homemade
2-3 cups of peeled, cubed kabocha or butternut squash
4-5 cups cooked heritage beans (or substitute bean mix of your choice)
1 (14 1/2-ounce) can chopped tomatoes
2 cups fresh or frozen corn kernels
cilantro for garnish

Season duck pieces or meat with cumin, salt, and pepper. Heat oil in a Dutch oven or large heavy-bottomed pan over medium-high heat until it shimmers. Add duck or meat, in batches if necessary, and cook, turning as needed, until lightly browned on all sides, 5 to 6 minutes. The fat that is rendered will add a delightful taste and richness to this dish. Transfer duck or meat to a bowl and set aside. Add onion and garlic to pan and sauté, stirring occasionally, until translucent, 5 to 7 minutes. Return duck or meat to pan, along with stock and squash, and bring to a boil. Reduce heat to medium-low and simmer, covered, for about 30 minutes. Add cooked beans, tomatoes, and corn; cook, uncovered, over medium heat until stew has thickened, about 40 minutes. Add cilantro and season to taste with salt and pepper.

Historic Table

Persimmon and Mesquite Pudding

The native American wild persimmon tree (*Diospyros virginiana*) grows from southern Connecticut to Florida and as far west as Kansas and Iowa. Like the pawpaw, wild persimmons have been foraged and cultivated as a food source by Native Americans since prehistoric days. Wild persimmons can be used for the following recipe. However, Fuyu persimmons are available seasonally. While "puddings" originated in England and were the earliest fillings for pies, this recipe will bake up more like a loaf than a custard. Mesquite flour was used widely by Indigenous Peoples of the Southwest and can be purchased online at casademesquite.com. If you cannot find it, just substitute any flour of your choice. This recipe is adapted from food.com.

2 1/4 cups all-purpose flour
1/4 cup mesquite flour
1/2 teaspoon baking soda
1 teaspoon baking powder
1 1/2 teaspoons salt
1 teaspoon ground cinnamon
1/2 teaspoon ground nutmeg
1 tablespoon freshly ground ginger
2 fresh eggs
3/4 cup sugar
1 cup peeled, cored, and pureed fresh Fuyu persimmons
1/4 cup buttermilk
1/2 cube melted unsalted butter
1 teaspoon vanilla extract

Sift together flours, baking soda and powder, salt, and spices. Set aside. In a separate bowl, beat eggs and sugar until light and fluffy. Add pureed persimmon and buttermilk and mix to combine. Stir in butter and vanilla. Grease a 9" x 5" loaf pan with spray, then line with parchment paper. Add liquid mixture to flour mixture and fold together gently. Transfer mixture into loaf pan. Bake at 325 degrees for 60-70 minutes until the center is set and sides begin to pull away from the pan. Check bread at about 30 minutes, and if it appears too dark, cover with foil for the remainder of the time. Test by pricking the center with a toothpick to be sure it comes out clean. Allow to cool before slicing. Serve warm with sweetened whipped cream or vanilla ice cream.

The Golden Age of Discovery

The world changed in 1492. Europeans and Native Americans alike were suddenly confronted with the realization that the world was much bigger than they could have imagined. The moment Christopher Columbus set foot in the Caribbean marked a turning point in history. It was one of those historical events, like the invention of the Gutenberg press or the signing of the Magna Carta, that marked the end of how things were and ushered in an entirely different reality.

Of course, no one living in 1492 knew the full extent of what lay ahead. Europeans greeted the news with enthusiasm, and an unprecedented era of discovery was soon underway. Explorers from Spain, Portugal, England, and other European nations soon financed expeditions to explore this "New World." Christian Europeans, conditioned by four centuries of the Crusades, saw this as an opportunity to spread their faith to vast new populations of potential converts. European adventurers, seeking the East's riches, suddenly had access to an unknown land that they expected was full of gold and treasure, not to mention the fabled fountain of youth!

The Native Nations, tribes, and peoples spread throughout the Americas would slowly face an unstoppable force of conquistadores, adventurers, and colonists. While Europeans saw a new era dawning, the Natives often faced death and the destruction of their ancient cultures and ways of life. Despite overwhelming odds, many Native nations persevered and preserved their culture.

We will now turn our attention to the determined man who set off this series of triumphal and cataclysmic events.

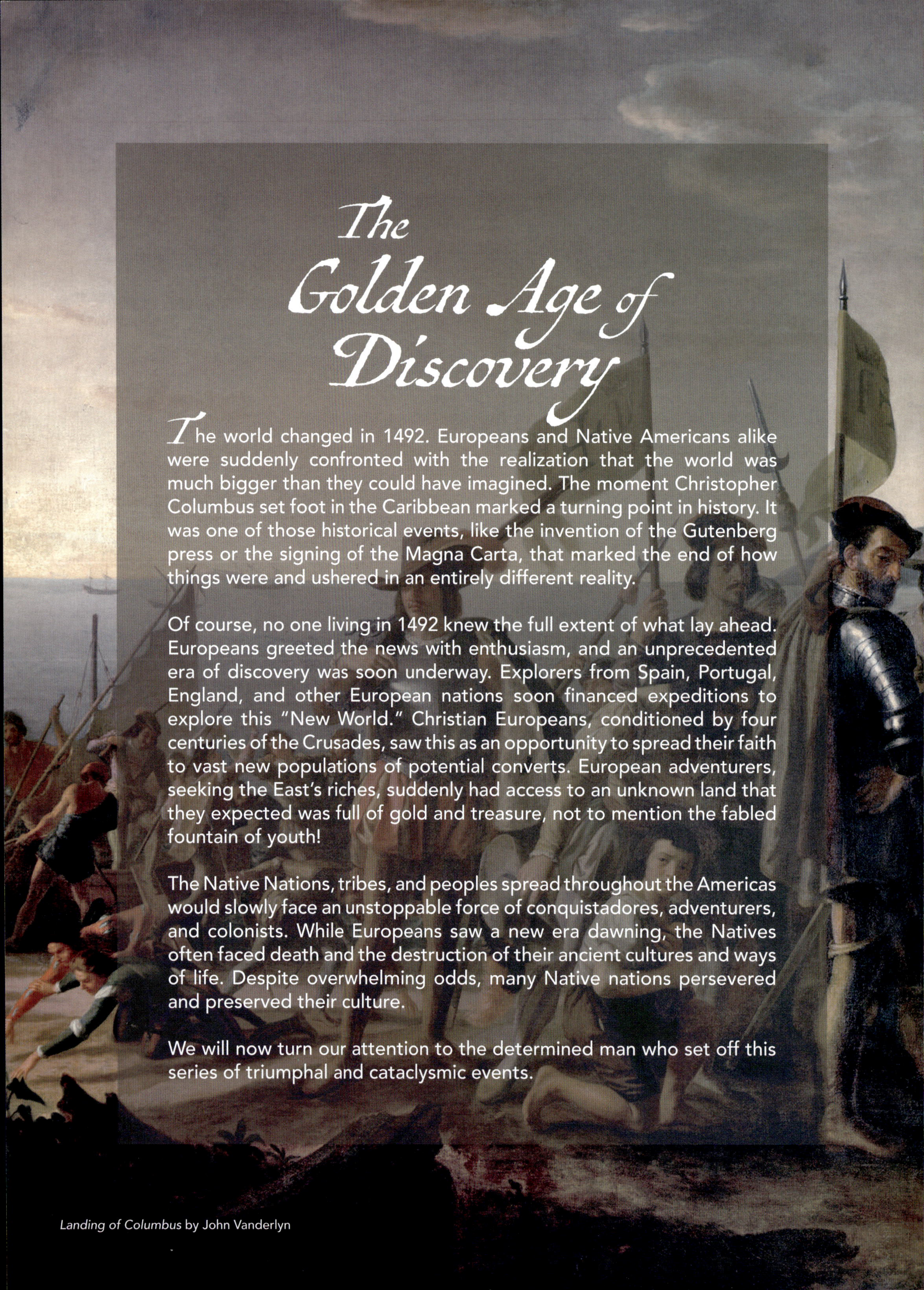

Landing of Columbus by John Vanderlyn

Rabbit Trails

Encounter by Jane Yolen
The Columbian conquest of the Taino people is told from the perspective of a young Taino boy, providing a needed balance to the standard European focus.

Exploration and Conquest: The Americas After Columbus 1500-1620 by Betsy and Giulio Maestro
The Maestros have compiled a much-needed primary history of the century after the Columbian discovery of America. This book provides a perspective of both the European settlers and the Native Peoples—whose lives were forever changed during the conquest.

Follow the Dream: The Story of Christopher Columbus by Peter Sis
Award-winning author and illustrator Peter Sis relates his coming to America from a country surrounded by an Iron Curtain, to the challenges Columbus faced as he sought to reach "the East by sailing west."

Around the World in a Hundred Years: From Henry the Navigator to Magellan by Jean Fritz
In her delightful and endearing way, beloved children's author Jean Fritz tells the stories of ten explorers who, between 1421 and 1522, ventured into the unknown.

Leif the Lucky and *Columbus* by Ingri and Edgar Parin D'Aulaire
The gorgeous lithographs and well-researched texts bring clarity and interest to these two intrepid and courageous explorers and they roles they played in the opening of the New World.

The King's Fifth by Scott O'Dell
While imprisoned and awaiting trial, Esteban, a seventeen-year-old cartographer, recalls his adventures with a band of conquistadors.

Crafts & Projects

Make a Model Fifteenth-Century Sailing Ship

Easy print-and-paste paper model *Santa Maria*: www.papertoys.com/santamaria.htm

Instructions for a wide variety of options for making replicas of Columbus's ships, including a ship in a bottle!
https://toy-models.wonderhowto.com/how-to/recreate-models-christopher-columbuss-sailing-ships-from-1492-0121462/

Make a Ship's Hourglass

Directions for making an hourglass out of jars (parental help required):
www.theshabbycreekcottage.com/diy-hourglass.html

Make an hourglass out of soda bottles:
www.wikihow.com/Make-a-Sand-Timer-from-Recycled-Plastic-Bottles

Write a News Broadcast

Instruct your student to write and act out a news broadcast for October 12, 1492. There will be several roles, so recruit siblings, family members, and friends. Roles to cast are newscaster, reporters, and witnesses/interviewees. Determine if the newscaster will report from the Taino or Spanish perspective. Include interviews with both Taino and Spanish witnesses. If desired, use costumes for added authenticity. Perform for family and friends.

Character Connection: Patience

Have your student define *patience* using a dictionary. Discuss the meaning of patience in the context of the following verses:

Proverbs 14:29	Proverbs 15:18	Proverbs 19:11
Proverbs 25:15	Ecclesiastes 7:8	Romans 12:12
1 Corinthians 13:4	Colossians 3:12	

As you read through these stories, look for examples of patience. When did someone demonstrate patience and understanding? How can patience produce understanding? What happens when someone lacks patience? People are complex and can be patient in some situations and impatient in others. Do you see any examples of this in these stories?

Christopher Columbus at the gates of the monastery of Santa Maria de la Rabida with his son Diego by Benito Mercade y Fabregas, 1858

LESSON 25

1. Have your student begin a new section in the notebook and title it "The Age of Discovery."

2. Read Chapter 2 of *A Child's First.*

   a. Christopher Columbus was named after Saint Christopher. If you are not familiar with this historical figure, the following website relates the story that Columbus would have heard from childhood: www.allpatronsaints.com/pages/st-christopher-the-patron-saint-of-travelers

   b. What innovation in sailing made Columbus's voyage possible? *The invention of the caravel.*

   c. Discuss Columbus's use of the word "childlike" to describe the Natives he met on the beach. Does this seem patronizing on Columbus's part? Do you agree or disagree with this description? Why or why not?

3. Have your student choose an activity from the Crafts and Projects section on page 39.

LESSON 26

1. Introduce *Where Do You Think You're Going, Christopher Columbus?* by Jean Fritz. Read through page 20.

   a. What happened in 1453 to stop trade between Europe and Asia? *The Islamic Turks, who had been at war with the Christian Europeans for centuries, gained control of the trade routes.*

   b. What explorer influenced Columbus's passion for traveling to Cipangu (Japan)? *Marco Polo.*

   c. Why did Columbus think that Queen Isabella of Spain would be more open to his ideas? *Columbus appealed to Isabella's religious passion, offering up the possibility of endless converts in Asia.*

   d. What words would you use to describe Christopher Columbus based upon our reading?

2. If desired, begin working on making replicas of the *Niña*, the *Pinta*, and the *Santa Maria*. Directions are linked in the Crafts and Projects section on page 39.

LESSON 27

1. Read through page 33 of *Where Do You Think You're Going, Christopher Columbus?*

   a. What do you think of the food the sailors ate while aboard Columbus's ships?

   b. How did Columbus attempt to ease his men's fears? Was this honest? *He did not accurately report the distance they sailed each day. He told them shorter distances so they would not feel as far from home. It was not honest.*

   c. How did Columbus treat Rodrigo, the sailor who first sighted land? *Columbus claimed that he had seen a fire on the land the night before and refused to give Rodrigo credit or the prize promised to the first person to sight land.*

   d. How did the Natives welcome Columbus and his men? *They were friendly and generous.*

2. Did you notice on page 33 the mention of mermaids or sea cows? These are manatees! Have your student cut out and color the manatee picture from the Picture Packet and paste it in the notebook along with a few key facts from your research.

LESSON 28

1. Read through page 49 of *Where Do You Think You're Going, Christopher Columbus?*

    a. Discuss how Columbus failed to adapt his understanding of the world as he encountered all sorts of things that did not line up with his expectations. Is it difficult to adjust to new ideas? Do you think this stubbornness will cost Columbus?

    b. Columbus secured funding from Queen Isabella by promising her two things: new converts to the Christian faith and gold. Did he succeed? Which objective did he spend the most time pursuing? *Columbus did not succeed on either front. He spent far more time asking the Native peoples about gold.*

    c. What happened on Christmas Day in 1492? Who helped the explorers? *Columbus's flagship, the* Santa Maria, *ran aground and had to be abandoned. The Native peoples helped Columbus and his men rescue everything they could from the ship.*

2. Caravels were crucial to the success of Columbus's mission to sail further from land than any European had before him. Learn more about these ships at the following website, and have your student record their findings in the notebook: www.history.com/news/christopher-columbus-ships-caravels

3. Begin working on painting a map of Columbus's first voyage. Have your student use the map on page 45 as a guide to paint a large map on butcher paper or construction paper using paints or watercolors. Once your student has finished constructing their model ship, they can place it on the map as a 3D representation of the voyage.

LESSON 29

1. Read through page 61 of *Where Do You Think You're Going, Christopher Columbus?*

    a. Describe Columbus's reception upon his return to Spain. *Columbus returned to grand celebrations and was an instant celebrity. The king and queen stood to greet him. He also received all the titles and honors he had demanded.*

    b. What did Columbus find upon his return to Hispaniola? *The Spaniards had treated one of the neighboring tribes terribly. The tribe had retaliated and killed the 39 Spaniards and burned their fort.*

    c. Did Columbus make promises to Queen Isabella that he had no way of keeping? *Yes, he promised 12 ships full of gold and spices, even though he had no evidence he could fulfill his pledge.*

    d. When Columbus could not find gold, what did he send to Spain instead? Discuss Columbus's character and what this decision reveals about him. *He captured 500 Native people to sell as slaves. Columbus, as we have seen, was unusually determined. While his tenacity propelled him to sail unknown waters, his pride would not allow him to admit his failure. His drive to become wealthy in the highly profitable slave trade blinded him to the humanity of the Taino.*

2. The people that Columbus encountered in the Caribbean were almost all Taino or Carib. They paid dearly for their encounter with the Spanish. Enslavement and exposure to disease resulted in such devastation that, for centuries, it was assumed that the Taino were the victims of genocide. Recent developments in DNA research have changed that history. Read more about the people proudly preserving their Taino heritage: www.nationalgeographic.com/history/2019/1a0/meet-survivors-taino-tribe-paper-genocide/

LESSON 30

1. Finish reading *Where Do You Think You're Going, Christopher Columbus?*

   a. Discuss Columbus's ideas about finding the Garden of Eden or Solomon's gold mines. Today that does not make any sense because we know he was in South America. But if you put yourself in Columbus's shoes, how does it become plausible? *Columbus did not know that North and South America existed, so he continued to operate under his assumption that he was in the East. As he progressed further west, he began to believe that he was nearing the Middle East, the land of the Bible.*

   b. John Cabot, Vasco da Gama, Ferdinand Magellan, and Amerigo Vespucci explored parts of the Americas for European crowns. Have your student choose one of these explorers to research and record key points in the notebook.

2. The following blog documents how the author educated her son about their Taino heritage and contains activities and helpful links:
https://discoveringtheworldthroughmysonseyes.com/category/discovering-our-taino-ancestry/

LESSON 31

1. Introduce *Pedro's Journal* by Pam Conrad. This book is written from the perspective of a ship's boy and scribe serving Columbus and presents a fresh viewpoint on the moral dilemmas faced by the expedition's members. Countering the narrative that Spanish mistreatment of the Natives was culturally acceptable at the time, it reveals that voices were speaking out, including Queen Isabella and Bartolome de las Casas. These opposing voices are revealed through the eyes of young Pedro, capturing the varied emotions and experiences of those who took part in this world-changing journey. Read pages 1-25.

   a. What was Pedro's job on the *Santa Maria*? *Pedro was a ship's boy charged with helping Columbus keep records.*

   b. On September 21, the ships sailed into a mass of seaweed known as the Sargasso Sea, the only sea not bordered by land. Learn more at the following sites:
   https://oceanservice.noaa.gov/facts/sargassosea.html
   www.atlasobscura.com/places/sargasso-sea

   c. Discuss what it must have been like to be a sailor on one of Columbus's ships. What would it have felt like to be surrounded by sea for weeks, with no concept of how long this voyage would take? Think about seeing your food and fresh water supplies running low. Would you be bored? Scared? Terrified? Discuss how difficult it is to enter fully into a fifteenth-century sailor's mindset. When the sailors were unable to measure the depth of the ocean, it was unnerving. Watch the following video to learn a bit more about ocean depth: "This Incredible Animation Shows How Deep the Ocean Really Is" on the Tech Insider YouTube channel.

2. Pedro is in charge of turning the ship's hourglass. Make one with your student. Refer to the directions linked on page 39.

3. The parrots that Pedro mentions were probably macaws. Cut out the blue and yellow macaws picture from the Picture Packet, and have your student add it to the notebook along with a few facts from your research.

LESSON 32

1. Read pages 26-43 of *Pedro's Journal.*

   a. Discuss why Columbus captured six men from the friendly tribe that greeted his arrival. What do you think motivated him? How was this a violation of the principle of imago Dei?

2. The green iguana would have been particularly surprising to the Spanish explorers. Cut out the iguana picture from the Picture Packet, and have your student color it and paste it into the notebook along with a few facts from your research.

LESSON 33

1. Read pages 44-54 of *Pedro's Journal.*

   a. These pages document how Columbus's growing frustration propelled the crew from one island to the next in a frenzy of claiming lands and searching for gold. Throughout history, land has been taken through war and conquest. Discuss how European and Native peoples' views of land "ownership" differed. How does conquest often violate the principle of imago Dei?

   b. How did the interactions between the Spanish and the Natives begin to change? *The Taino stopped greeting the arrival of the Spanish with joy and gifts. They hid or fled whenever the explorers approached.*

2. Have your student cut out, color, and paste the Columbus picture on the timeline.

LESSON 34

1. Finish reading *Pedro's Journal.*

   a. Pedro begins his journey with Columbus as a proud, naïve boy ready for adventure. How would you describe him at the end of the book?

2. Columbus was a complex historical character who changed the world. The debate around how to remember him is active and vigorous. Host a mock trial in which your student takes turns defending and prosecuting Columbus.

LESSON 35

1. Once Columbus landed in the Caribbean, it would never be the same. A flood of explorers, missionaries, and conquistadors followed. Read Chapter 3 of *A Child's First.*

   a. Why did Spain go to such great lengths to explore the Americas? *Spain had depleted its treasury in expelling the Moors from its borders. The allure of gold was irresistible, and Spain wanted to beat the rest of Europe to claim all the treasures of this land for itself. It seems that they failed to see the irony between expelling their own invaders and invading other lands themselves.*

   b. How was De Soto able to deceive the Natives into thinking he was a god? *Besides telling them that he was a god, he performed tricks to back up his claim. He said a mirror allowed him to see into the future and to read people's thoughts. De Soto took advantage of an old legend that foretold the coming of a white conqueror.*

2. The story of Álvar Núñez Cabeza de Vaca is remarkable. Access a video about his years-long journey of survival and how it changed him. Search "The Incredible Journey of Cabeza De Vaca (1527-1536) on the History Time YouTube Channel. See Rabbit Trails for an excellent title on de Vaca.

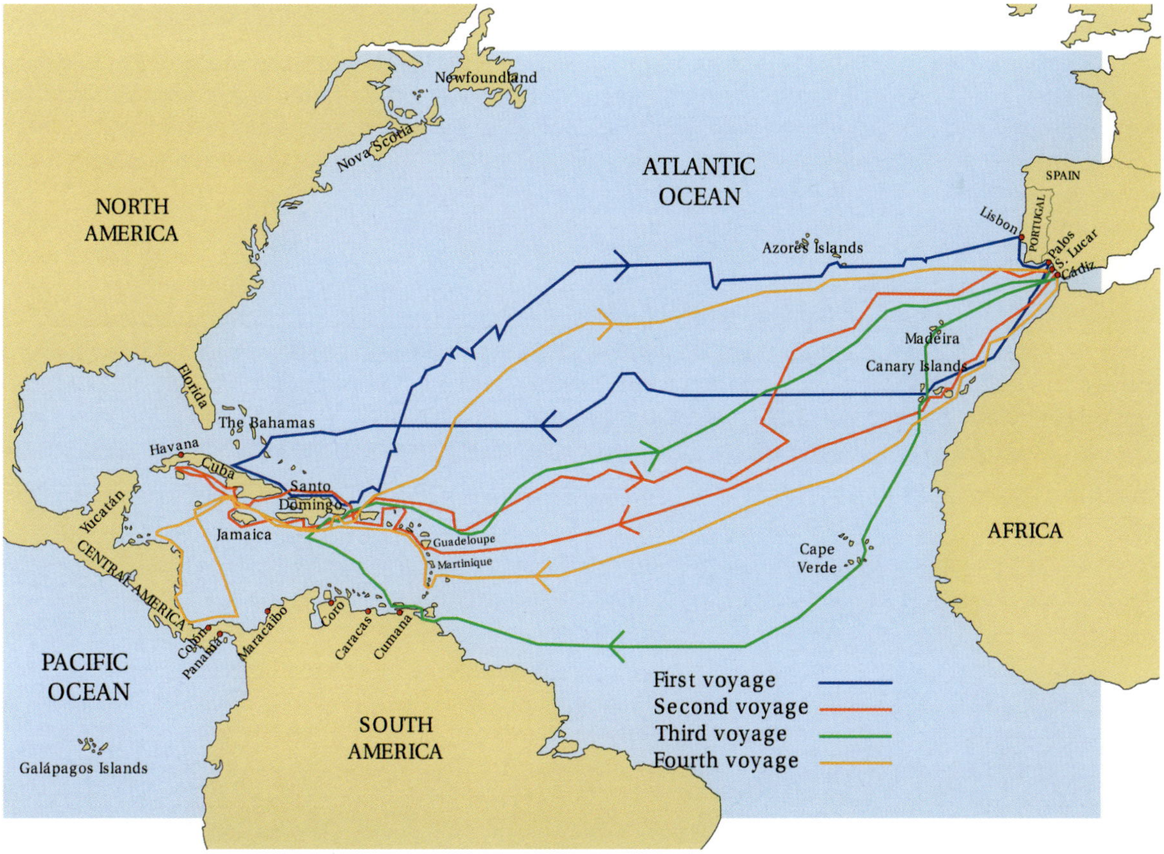

1. Taino zemi sculpture. 2. Green iguana. 3. Columbus's four voyages to the Americas.

Historic Table

Leek Soup or Pottage de Porrada

This fifteenth-century Catalan recipe would have been familiar to most Spanish sailors who braved the Atlantic crossing during the Golden Age of Discovery. Simple but tasty, this is especially fitting for a cold winter night. The Spanish brought the potato (which they discovered in Peru) to Europe in the 1530s. Almond milk was used in the original fifteenth-century recipe, so those with dairy sensitivities can make this truly authentic! I have substituted whole milk. Coconut cream can be substituted for the half-and-half. This recipe is adapted from one on medievalcuisine.com.

2 pounds leeks, cleaned, and sliced thinly
2 1/2 cups almond or whole milk
1 pound bacon
1 quart chicken broth
6 garlic cloves, minced
6 medium potatoes, peeled and cubed
1 cup half-and-half
2 tablespoons chopped parsley
1 teaspoon herbes de Provence
1/2 cup white wine (optional)
freshly ground pepper
sea salt to taste

The trick to cooking with leeks is proper cleaning beforehand. Large leeks can store dirt in between the multiple layers and need to be carefully washed. Peel dark green outer layers and discard. Use the light green and white portions. Best results are achieved by slicing leeks first, then plunging them in cold water to soak. Stir vigorously to dislodge dirt and rinse in a colander under running water. Dry leeks.

In a large Dutch oven or pot, cook bacon until crisp. Remove bacon from the pot. Sauté sliced leeks and garlic in bacon fat until tender. Add broth, herbs, potatoes, and pepper and simmer over low heat for about 1 hour. Add almond milk or milk and half-and-half to soup and cook until desired thickness of pottage is reached. At this stage, the soup can be partly creamed with an immersion blender, leaving some chunkiness for texture. Add salt to taste. Crumble cooked bacon and add it with the chopped parsley to the soup. Serve with hot crusty sourdough or French bread.

The Mayflower Compact by N. C. Wyeth, 1938

The Colonies

Europeans waited expectantly for reports from the explorers they had sent across the Atlantic. Tales of open space, fabled fountains of youth, and opportunities to start a new life poured back and set off a wave of early colonial exploration and settlement. As we saw in the Indigenous Peoples section of this study, what many Europeans saw as a vast "virgin" territory replete with resources and possibilities was already settled by Native tribes and nations. Despite this reality, the colonization efforts of Spain, France, England, the Dutch Republic, and others moved forward throughout the late-sixteenth and early-seventeenth centuries.

In the earliest days of colonization, the English claimed the northeastern coasts, while Spanish explorers planted their flag in Florida and the lands surrounding the Gulf of Mexico. New Amsterdam, which eventually became New York, was settled as a Dutch trading post. France laid claim to the vast Louisiana Territory. European monarchs sponsored these earliest settlements, looking to expand their empires and reap the riches available in the Americas. Adventurers and noblemen came in search of wealth and fame.

As more of this world was mapped and settled, a new wave of immigrants seeking religious freedom and escaping the rigid class systems of Europe made their way across the vast Atlantic. Quakers, Separatists, and Puritans came to Pennsylvania and Massachusetts. Maryland was founded as a refuge for British Roman Catholics, and Georgia was colonized by the "worthy poor"—unemployed British citizens led by James Oglethorpe. This complex mix of backgrounds and motivations resulted in wide-ranging outcomes for the colonists themselves and for the Indigenous Peoples who occupied these lands.

There are inspiring stories of those who came with a genuine belief in the imago Dei of the Indigenous People of North America. The Separatists who settled Plimoth Plantation, William Penn in Pennsylvania, and James Oglethorpe in Georgia offer examples of colonists who followed the Golden Rule with their Native neighbors.

Sadly, there are many examples of injustices where entire Native populations were displaced, and their lands were stolen. This tragedy would unfold over decades and centuries. We will learn more about both the good and the bad of the colonial period in our readings, so let's turn our attention to Jamestown, established by the English on May 4, 1607.

Rabbit Trails

The Struggle for a Continent: The French and Indian Wars 1689-1763
by Betsy and Giulio Maestro
The French and Indian Wars were a tumultuous time in America's early history and involved not only the colonial forces from France but also many Indigenous tribes, as well as England and even George Washington.

The New Americans: Colonial Times–1620-1689
by Betsy and Giulio Maestro
The Colonial era in America saw eager settlers from all over Europe come to build new lives in this foreign place. Finns, Swedes, Dutch, English, French, and Spanish all vied for places to make their own.

Molly Bannaky by Alice McGill
In 1683 Molly Walsh was a poor milkmaid in England when she was sold into indenture in the new colony of Maryland. Working tobacco, Molly learned the hardships of long days slaving in the hot sun.

Homes in the Wilderness:
A Pilgrim's Journal of Plymouth Plantation in 1620
by William Bradford
The fascinating story of the Pilgrims' first winter in Massachusetts is told here through the journal of William Bradford.

The Lost Colony of Roanoke by Jean Fritz
When an archeological dig was scheduled to take place at Cape Hatteras, Jean Fritz called her archeologist friend and asked to go.

Colonial Craftsmen and the Beginnings of Industry by Edwin Tunis
America's colonial craftsmen, with their resourcefulness, ingenuity, and skill, were a group of "liberty-loving artisans" who included the blacksmith, cooper, joiner, weaver, cordwainer, housewright, and countless others.

Recommended Readers

A Lion to Guard Us by Clyde Robert Bulla

Calico Bush by Rachel Field

The Sign of the Beaver
by Elizabeth George Speare

Calico Captive
by Elizabeth George Speare

The Witch of Blackbird Pond
by Elizabeth George Speare

The Double Life of Pocahontas
by Jean Fritz

Indian Captive: The Story of Mary Jemison
by Lois Lenski

Online Resources

The Powhatan and their culture: www.historyisfun.org/learn/learning-center/who-were-the-powhatan-indians-and-how-did-they-live-2/

"'People of the River: Powhatan Indians' Henricus Historical Park Educational film" on the LionHeart FilmWorks YouTube channel

The Lost Colony of Roanoke is a puzzle that has fascinated historians for centuries. In 2020 archaeologists working in North Carolina believed they may have found an explanation! Read about it at the following links:

www.nationalgeographic.co.uk/history-and-civilisation/2017/11/first-english-settlers-survived-and-joined-native-americans

www.nationalgeographic.com/history/2020/11/newfound-survivor-camp-may-explain-lost-colony-roanoke/

Watch the following videos from the Fairfax Network–Fairfax County Public Schools YouTube channel to learn more about how language and culture made communication between the English and the Powhatan people challenging:

"Virginia's First People: The Powhatan–The Language Barrier"

"Virginia's First People: The Powhatan–The Culture Barrier"

Learn about the Mayflower Compact: "The Pilgrims: Mayflower Compact" at pbslearningmedia.org/collection/americanexperiencethepilgrims/

Take virtual field trips of Plimoth Plantation. These engaging videos allow you to tour the Mayflower, meet Wampanoag and Pilgrim actors, and more. The virtual tours are available on Scholastic's YouTube channel: "Plimoth Plantation: Virtual Field Trip"

Watch a video on William Penn: "In Penn's Shadow: Philadelphia: the Great Experiment" available on YouTube.

Benjamin West and His Cat Grimalkin
by Marguerite Henry

This is the delightful story of the Quaker boy who loved to paint so much that "he dug his colors out of the earth and made his brushes from his cat's tail." Unfortunately for Benjamin, Quakers forbade the creation of "images" and paintings were seen as worldly distractions. This presented Benjamin's father with a thorny religious problem. Happily, for posterity, the Quaker leadership recognized the beauty of West's gift and voted to allow him to study art. As a child, Benjamin learned from Native Americans how to make paints by mixing clay and bear grease, and he never forgot his humble beginnings. He maintained to the end of his life that "a kiss from my mother made me a painter." Benjamin went on to become a court painter for King George III, the only American ever appointed president of the Royal Academy of England, and is known as the father of American painting.

Crafts & Projects

Character Connection: Faith

Use the following verses to discuss the concept of faith as you read through the literature selections. Faithfulness to God drove the Pilgrims to leave everything they knew. Belief in imago Dei led William Penn to found a colony established in peaceful relationship with the Lenape. Amos Fortune's faith led him to lead a life of integrity and sacrificial generosity. Where else do you see faithfulness exhibited in these stories? Are there examples of being unfaithful? What are the results? The Bible often talks about the faithfulness of God. Can you see examples of His faithfulness in the lives of the people we are learning about?

Proverbs 3:3-4
Proverbs 21:21
Romans 12:3
1 Corinthians 16:13
1 Timothy 6:11-12
James 1:8
James 2:17
2 Peter 1: 5-7

Practice being an archaeologist

Much of what we know about early colonies like Roanoke and Jamestown as well as the Indigenous inhabitants comes to us through archaeologists' work. Learn more about this science with the following activities:

What is an artifact? Discover how everyday objects become artifacts:
https://historicjamestowne.org/wp-content/uploads/What-is-an-Artifact.pdf

Create an Archaeological Dig
Prep without students: paint designs on two or three old clay pots. Gather a couple of old ceramic plates or bowls. A thrift store is a great place to get these. Place pots and plates/bowls in a large paper bag and gently hit it with a hammer. Remove about half of the pieces—especially any sharp ones—and place the remaining "artifacts" in a sandbox or tray filled with dirt or sand. Give your students gloves to protect their hands, as well as shovels, paintbrushes, and other tools. Have them work carefully to find the artifacts and work on piecing the pieces together. The fact that some of the pieces are missing will add to the challenge as well as the authenticity of the project.

Learn more about archaeology here:
https://ask.mrdonn.org/archaeology/

Pretend to be a colonist

What would it have felt like to leave everything you know to make a home in a place that was unmapped and had no houses, shops, grocery stores, or Home Depots? The colonists had to start with nothing and even establish their own governing rules.

What would you pack? www.historyisfun.org/lesson5/

How will you get to Virginia? The following PDF has information on the voyage and instructions on how to tie nautical knots and pass the time with a popular dice game: www.historyisfun.org/wp-content/uploads/2014/05/AA_Ship-Activity-sheets.pdf

What are the rules of this new colony? The following traces the development of colonial government with examples of specific laws. These laws are a lot of fun to discuss. www.historyisfun.org/laws-at-jamestown/

Learn about traditional food preservation methods used by colonists and Powhatan alike:
www.historyisfun.org/wp-content/uploads/2014/09/AnnasAdventures_Food_4pages.pdf

Mapmaking was an essential aspect of colonization. Learn more here:
www.historyisfun.org/wp-content/uploads/2014/09/Mapmaking_Activity.pdf

Solve a Thanksgiving mystery in Massachusetts as you learn about the Wampanoag and the Pilgrims

https://youarethehistorian.org/#/intro

LESSON 36

1. Read Chapter 4 of *A Child's First.*

    a. What were some of the reasons Britain chose to start a colony in America? *Britain wanted to turn the natural resources of the New World into wealth back home. It also wanted to prevent Spain from laying claim to this new territory. The Church of England also wanted to spread Christianity to the Natives, and many Englishmen wanted adventure, freedom, and the opportunity to start a new life.*

    b. Why is Jamestown called "the cradle of our liberties"? Jamestown was built on what principles? *Jamestown was the first permanent English settlement, and it is remembered as the cradle of our liberties for legislating the following: 1) Respect for church and God, 2) trial by jury, and in time, 3) representative government.*

    c. What obstacles did the British face in Jamestown? *Jamestown colonists faced infighting, disease, shortages of food and supplies, and attacks from the Powhatan people.*

2. Have your student begin a new section in the notebook titled "The Colonies." The first colony featured in this section will be Jamestown. Have your student cut out the Chesapeake Bay region map from the Picture Packet and paste it into the notebook. Label the following:

Atlantic Ocean	Jamestown	Roanoke
Chesapeake Bay		

LESSON 37

1. We will now learn about the Jamestown colony, which was established in the territory of the Powhatan people. This confederation of thirty Algonquian-speaking tribes was ruled by Wahunsenacawh, Pocahontas's father! The English called him Powhatan, which was one of his many titles. To avoid confusion, Powhatan will be referred to by this title, and the people will be referred to as the Powhatan people.

2. Introduce *Pocahontas and the Strangers* by Clyde Robert Bulla. Read Chapters 1-4.

    a. Were the Jamestown settlers the first white people to come to the land of the Powhatan people? *No. There had been previous exploratory visits and attempts at colonization, but they had all failed.*

3. The eagle that Pocahontas rescued was a golden eagle. Cut out the golden eagle picture from the Picture Packet, and have your student add it to the notebook along with a few facts about these birds of prey.

LESSON 38

1. Read Chapters 5-8 of *Pocahontas and the Strangers.*

    a. Why were the Powhatan people uneasy about the intentions of the settlers? *They believed that the settlers would attack them.*

2. The only firsthand historical account of Pocahontas rescuing John Smith comes from Smith himself. The lack of collaborative accounts has caused some to question the story. If desired, research this historical controversy. Once the research is complete, have your student write or narrate the event twice: once from Pocahontas's perspective and once from John Smith's. Discuss the importance of multiple eyewitness accounts both in supporting history and in the courtroom. See the following scriptures: Deut. 19:15, 2 Cor. 13:1.

3. The historical site where John Smith met Powhatan has been recently discovered! Learn about it at the following link, and have your student mark this geographical site on the map in the notebook:
www.nps.gov/cajo/planyourvisit/werowocomoco.htm

1. *The Coronation of Powhatan* by John Gadsby Chapman, 1835.
2. Algonquian village of Pomeoic, 1585.

LESSON 39

1. Read Chapters 9-12 of *Pocahontas and the Strangers.*

    a. Pocahontas and her brother, Nantaquas, argued about the intentions of the settlers. Discuss this disagreement from both perspectives.

2. Have your student cut out, color, and paste the Jamestown picture on the timeline.

3. Choose an activity from the Crafts and Projects or Online Resources, pages 51-52, to enjoy with your student.

LESSON 40

1. Read Chapters 13-17 of *Pocahontas and the Strangers.*

    a. Tom Savage stated that the English colonists sent to work in the Powhatan village "would like to stay always." As more and more colonists settled in North America, a phenomenon occurred that surprised the English. Some colonists decided to leave their fellow Englishmen to assimilate with the Indigenous Tribes. It became such a problem at different points that laws were passed forbidding colonists from leaving their settlements. Ben Franklin wrote, "No European who has tasted Savage Life can afterwards bear to live in our societies." Discuss this phenomenon.

    b. How did Pocahontas help the English once again? *She warned them of Powhatan's plan to attack.*

2. Learn more about the Jamestown settlement by visiting historicjamestowne.org. Have your student research Captain John Smith's life and record key points in the notebook.

3. White-tailed deer were common in the Powhatan territories and provided food, leather for clothing, bowstrings, and more. Cut out the white-tailed deer picture from the Picture Packet, and have your student color and add it to the notebook along with a few facts from your research.

LESSON 41

1. Finish reading *Pocahontas and the Strangers.*

    a. What aspects of Pocahontas's life do you find most remarkable?

    b. Pocahontas's life has traditionally been viewed as heroic by Americans, but the Powhatan people have a different perspective and see her life as a cautionary tale. Discuss how Pocahontas's role in saving the Jamestown colony would have been viewed by the Powhatan. Discuss her actions both from the perspective of the Powhatan people and the Jamestown settlers. How does a shift in perspective reframe Pocahontas's actions?

2. Pocahontas's visit to England took place in 1616, the same year Claes Van Visscher produced an engraved panorama of London (see the following pages). This coincidence allows us to peek at London and see what Pocahontas would have seen. You can also see an updated engraving of the London skyline produced in 2016 to commemorate the 400th anniversary of the original artwork here: www.theguardian.com/cities/2016/mar/03/london-skyline-1616-2016-interactive-faders-visscher

LESSON 42

1. We will now move north from Virginia to the area we now know as New England to study the Pilgrims. Read Chapter 5 of *A Child's First.*

2. Have your student trace or cut out the North Atlantic area map in the Picture Packet. Color the map and illustrate, if desired, and add it to the notebook. Label:

Plymouth, England	London	Atlantic Ocean
Plymouth, Massachusetts	Cape Cod	Cape Cod Bay
Provincetown	Boston	

LESSON 43

1. Introduce *The Landing of the Pilgrims* by James Daugherty. Read pages 1-17.

   a. Have your student copy into the notebook William's response to his family when they tried to convince him not to join the Separatist Church:

   "To keep a good conscience and walk in such Way as God had prescribed in his Word, is a thing which I must prefer before you all, and above life itself. Wherefore, since it is for a good Cause that I am likely to suffer the disasters which you lay before me, you have no cause to be either angry with me, or sorry for me. Yea, I am not only willing to part with everything that is dear to me in this world for this Cause, but I am thankful that God hath given me heart so to do; and will accept me so to suffer for him."

   b. Learn about Master Brewster's Geneva Bible by reading about it on page 58.

2. Read more about the Pilgrims' time in Leiden and see photos of this beautiful city:
www.smithsonianmag.com/travel/the-pilgrims-before-plymouth-111851259

Panorama of London by Claes Van Visscher, 1616

LESSON 44

1. Read pages 18-31 of *The Landing of the Pilgrims.*

   a. What were some of the political and social reasons the Separatists chose to go to America? *The Pilgrims had several reasons for deciding to go to America: Holland's peace treaty with Spain was ending; the King of England had spies looking for the Separatists and had already shut down Mr. Brewster's printing press; many of the Separatists were assimilating into Dutch culture and forgetting their English roots; few Hollanders had converted to the Separatists' beliefs.*

   b. Dorothy and William Bradford discussed the need to "found a new state" on page 20. Discuss how the oppressive actions of the English government forced this realization. *The English had no freedom of the press and were persecuted for worshiping outside England's official church.*

   c. The Dutch made the Pilgrims a very generous offer to pay for their passage to the Island of Manhattan if they would settle in the Dutch colony there. Why did the Pilgrims turn down this opportunity? What was the result? *The Pilgrims were as proud of their English heritage as they were committed to their faith—the two were intertwined. To pay for their passage to an English colony, the Pilgrims had to agree to work four days per week for seven years to repay the merchants who underwrote the voyage and settlement.*

   d. Have your student narrate the troubles the Pilgrims had with the *Speedwell.*

2. Have your student research Bradford's life in preparation for writing a report or creating a presentation. Consider how his leadership skills led the colony to success.

V OF LONDON, 1616

The Geneva Bible

The Geneva Bible (1583) was a monumental achievement of the Reformation, produced fifty-one years before the more famous King James Version, which quickly overshadowed it and obscured its vital importance in history and literature. The Geneva Bible achieved remarkable things: accessibility, both physical and intellectual. It was the first mechanically produced English Bible and was therefore widely available. Next, it included study notes, maps, commentaries, and other tools to facilitate reading by laypersons. Chapter and verse numbers were used for the first time in an English Bible. The Bible was produced by Protestant English scholars who fled to Geneva, Switzerland, to escape persecution under Queen Mary I. These scholars, including John Calvin and John Knox, added extensive marginal notes and cross-referenced verses to help readers interpret and comprehend the scriptures.

The Geneva Bible would eventually make its way to Massachusetts aboard the *Mayflower*. It also shaped the language of William Shakespeare, John Bunyan, and John Milton!

To learn a bit more about this historic Bible, watch the following clip from *Pawn Stars* (of all shows!) to see examples of the marginal notes and view a copy of the 1583 Geneva Bible:

"Pawn Stars: 1583 Geneva Bible (Season 15) | History" on the Pawn Stars YouTube channel

1. Geneva Bible printed in Amsterdam in 1633. 2. Geneva Bible, 1560.

LESSON 45

1. Read pages 33-45 of *The Landing of the Pilgrims.*

   a. Why was the child born on the *Mayflower* named Oceanus? *Oceanus is the Latin word for "out of" or "from the ocean," so it was an appropriate name for a child born on the vast Atlantic.*

   b. Why did the Pilgrims choose to settle on Cape Cod? *There was a southerly wind that would not allow them to sail south.*

2. Chart on the map in the notebook the *Mayflower*'s journey from Plymouth, England, to the tip of Cape Cod. Also, mark the dates of its departure and arrival.

LESSON 46

1. Have your student copy the Mayflower Compact from pages 44-45 of *Landing of the Pilgrims* into the notebook.

2. Discuss the challenges of creating a new government. Working with your class or family, create a "charter" like the Mayflower Compact to govern your classroom or family. Propose rules and vote on them. Once the group has decided on rules, record them, and post them in the classroom. This exercise introduces the challenges of creating a government. Then-Massachusetts Governor Calvin Coolidge commemorated the 300th anniversary of the *Mayflower* landing and captured the importance of this event:

> The compact which they signed was an event of the greatest importance. It was the foundation of liberty based on law and order, and that tradition has been steadily upheld. They drew up a form of government which has been designated as the first real constitution of modern times. It was democratic, an acknowledgment of liberty under law and order and the giving to each person the right to participate in the government, while they promised to be obedient to the laws.
>
> But the really wonderful thing was that they had the power and strength of character to abide by it and live by it from that day to this. Some governments are better than others. But any form of government is better than anarchy, and any attempt to tear down government is an attempt to wreck civilization.

3. Read pages 46–55 of *The Landing of the Pilgrims.*

   a. What things did the scouting party find? *The scouting party found a field where the Patuxet had grown corn, an old lodge made of boards, Patuxet mounds with buried corn, two canoes, and a deer trap.*

   b. Why was Elder Brewster uneasy about what the scouting party did? *Brewster knew it was wrong to dig up Indian graves and take the buried corn. But he assured himself and others that once they met with the Natives, they would "give them full satisfaction." In other words, they would pay for the corn.*

1. Samoset appears at Plymouth. 2. *Massasoit, Great Sachem of the Wampanoag, Friend and Protector of the Pilgrims, 1621* sculpture by Cyrus E. Dallin in Kansas City, Missouri. 3. *The Departure of the Mayflower* by N. C. Wyeth, 1941.

LESSON 47

1. Read pages 56–69 of *The Landing of the Pilgrims.*

    a. What were some natural features that made Plymouth a suitable place to settle? *Plymouth was suitable because it had a good vantage point of the harbor for defense and a brook beside the settlement, and old Patuxet cornfields nearby meant fertile soil.*

    b. Discuss the toll that sickness, exposure, and hunger took on the Pilgrims during the first winter. Amid these hardships, who did William Bradford acknowledge for their selfless servitude and care for the sick and dying? *Bradford wrote that only six or seven people were well enough to tend the sick, most notably William Brewster and Miles Standish. These few men took it upon themselves to wash, feed, bathe, and tenderly care for the sick and dying.*

2. On pages 68-69 of *The Landing of the Pilgrims*, the author meditates on the cost of freedom. Discuss this. What were the Pilgrims willing to sacrifice for religious freedom? What do you think of the cost they paid?

3. Pilgrims saw wild turkeys for the first time as they built their settlement. Cut out the wild turkey picture from the Picture Packet, and have your student add it to the notebook along with a few facts from your research.

4. Have your student continue working on their report on William Bradford.

LESSON 48

1. Read pages 70–87 of *The Landing of the Pilgrims.*

    a. How did Samoset learn to speak English? *The fishermen who came each year to fish in the area had taught Samoset to speak English.*

    b. With whom did the Pilgrims make peace? How long did this treaty last? *The Pilgrims established peace with Massasoit and his tribe, which lasted for nearly 50 years.*

    c. The Pilgrims are shocked when Samoset comes into their settlement and greets them in English. To learn more about Samoset, visit www.notablebiographies.com/supp/Supplement-Mi-So/Samoset.html

2. Have your student cut out, color, and paste the Pilgrims picture onto the timeline.

3. Choose an activity from the Crafts and Projects or Online Resources (pages 51-52) to enjoy with your student.

LESSON 49

1. Read pages 88–100 of *The Landing of the Pilgrims.*

    a. Have your student narrate what happened when the Englishmen met Massasoit.

    b. Describe how Squanto was so integral to the success of the Plymouth Colony. Squanto's knowledge of the local tribes and his skills in hunting, trapping, fishing, and planting methods enabled the Pilgrims to survive the harsh winters. His knowledge of English and the local languages made him invaluable as an interpreter.

2. These chapters communicate the Pilgrim's perceptions of the Wampanoag and convey some of the cultural challenges facing both groups. Visit the following website to compare how the Pilgrims and Wampanoag lived: https://thekidshouldseethis.com/post/wampanoag-and-pilgrim-women-1620s-video

Coming of the Mayflower by N. C. Wyeth

LESSON 50

1. Read pages 101–114 of *The Landing of the Pilgrims.*

    a. How did Canonicus describe the gunpowder that Bradford stuffed into the snakeskin? *"It is the terrible medicine with which the English destroy our people and take from us the lands of our fathers."*

    b. How long did the Thanksgiving feast last? *Three days.*

    c. The background behind Squanto's attempts to turn the English against the Wampanoag is a bit complicated. If desired, learn more here: https://historyofmassachusetts.org/squanto-the-former-slave/

2. Have your student finish writing their report on William Bradford and add it to the notebook.

3. Lobsters were so prevalent in the early days of English colonization of New England, they were used as fertilizer, to feed prisoners, and generally thought of as a nuisance. Cut out the American lobster picture from the Picture Packet and have your student add it to the notebook along with a few facts.

LESSON 51

1. Finish reading *The Landing of the Pilgrims.*

    a. How did the Pilgrims demonstrate Christian charity to the passengers aboard the *Charity* and *Swan*? *Though the Pilgrims barely had enough provisions for themselves, they warmly welcomed the new arrivals and shared their meager supplies with them.*

    b. How did Captain Standish and his soldiers prevent the Witawamat's planned attack? *Captain Standish and his soldiers killed Witawamat and his men in a surprise attack. Witawamat was the leading agitator who convinced other tribes to unite against the English. By killing Witawamat, the Pilgrims averted the attack and caused the other tribes to back down.*

    c. How did the Pilgrims respond to the summer drought? *They set aside a day of prayer to humble themselves and thank God for His blessings.*

    d. Describe how free enterprise helped the Plymouth Colony. *When the colony decided that each family would be responsible for their own corn crop, the results were wonderful. People began working for themselves and not for the "community," which empowered each to take ownership in planting, tending, and guarding their crops.*

2. The final quotation in the book is from a letter that William Brewster wrote to Sir Edwin Sandys (a London financier) when the Pilgrims were considering moving from Holland to the New World. The rest of the quote is added below. Discuss how the Pilgrims demonstrated the truth of this belief in the successful establishment of the Plymouth Colony. If desired, have the student copy this quote in the student notebook.

    It is not with us as with other men whom small things can discourage, or small discontentments cause to wish themselves at home again. We believe and trust that the Lord is with us, unto whom and whose service we have given ourselves, and that he will graciously prosper our endeavors according to the simplicity of our hearts therein. —William Brewster

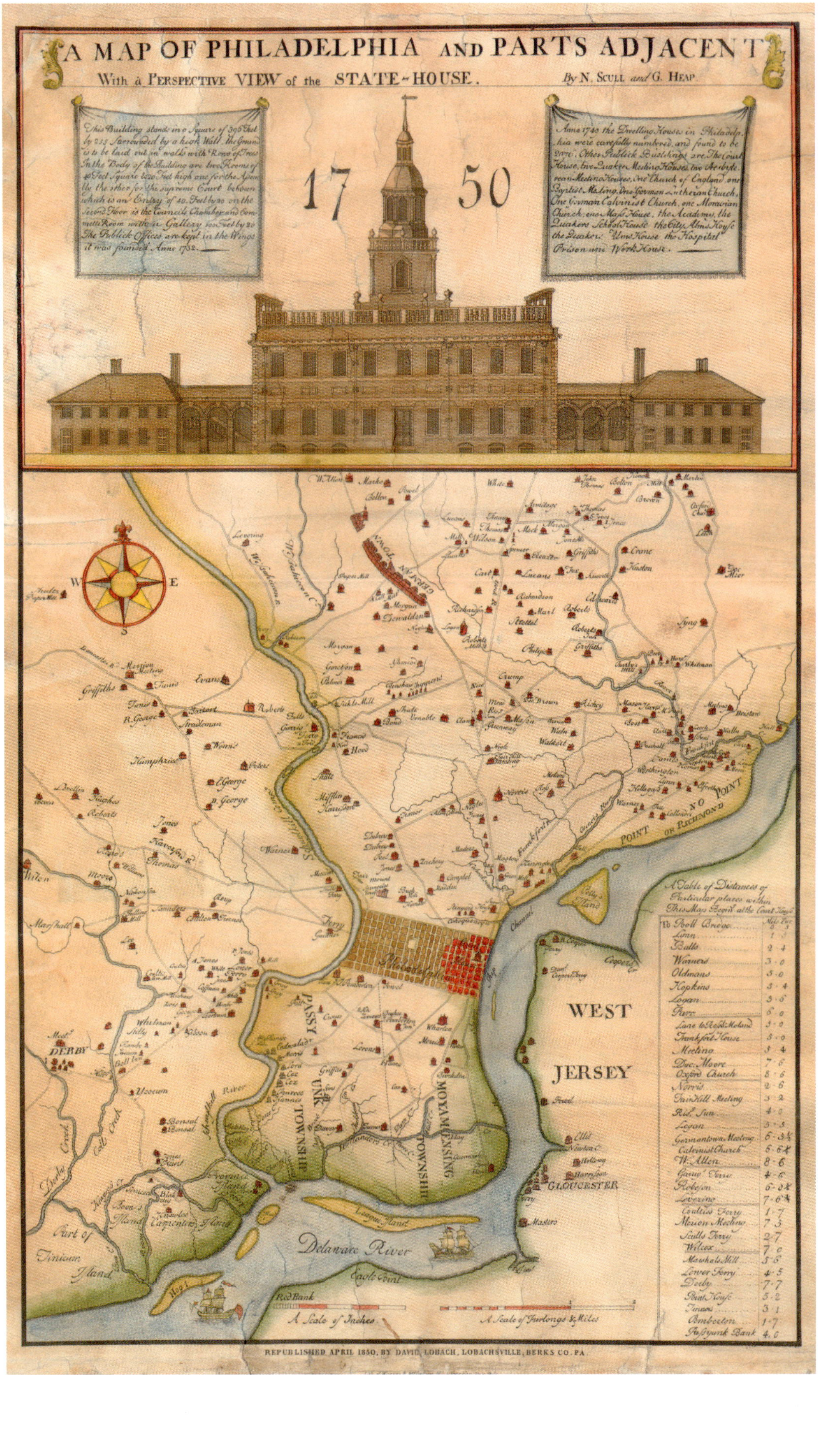

An 18th-century map of Philadelphia, circa 1752

LESSON 52

1. There were many similarities between the English colonies in Virginia and Massachusetts and some key differences. These characteristics would shape the thirteen colonies and their eventual battle against England for freedom. Watch the following videos to learn more: "Society and Religion in the New England Colonies" and "Politics and Native Relations in the New England Colonies" at khanacademy.org

2. Introduce *The World of William Penn* by Genevieve Foster. Note: This book covers world history during the lifetime of William Penn. Some sections will, therefore, be skipped to keep the focus on American history. The skipped sections are still recommended and provide excellent global context, but notes are not provided for those pages. Read pages 8-20 and discuss the following:

a. Why did the Quakers of England desire to immigrate to America? *In Britain, everyone had to attend the Church of England. For following their faith, the Quakers were subjected to fines, imprisonment, torture, and sometimes death.*

b. Why was William Penn expelled from Oxford? *William Penn refused to go along with some of the university's religious rules, resulting in his expulsion.*

c. When Penn was studying law in London, why were the schools shut down? How were the poor treated during the shutdown? How did the Quakers respond? *The Great Plague hit London, shutting down everything. The poor were locked in their homes to prevent the spread of the disease. The Quakers went about delivering food and caring for the sick, which touched William deeply.*

LESSON 53

1. Read pages 21-52 of *The World of William Penn.*

a. What happened to Penn in Ireland that dramatically changed his life? *At a Quaker meeting Penn attended in Cork, he heard a preacher speak of an "inner power that comes to each person directly from God—a kind of Inner Light to guide him through life." Penn was so convinced he had found the "inner light" that he submitted to arrest along with his fellow Quakers.*

b. What extraordinary event happens during Penn's trial for "disturbing the peace"? *Although the Magna Carta guaranteed the right to a jury trial for the accused, the law had been so perverted that most judges told the jury exactly how to vote. If a jurist defied the judge, he might suffer imprisonment himself. But Penn's jury listened to his plea to stand for their rights, which they did, establishing a landmark case in English justice.*

c. Who founded the Quaker religion? Describe how the name "Quaker" originated. What did the Boston Puritans do to the Quakers when they arrived in their colony? *George Fox was the founder of the Quaker faith. When arrested for preaching, he responded to the officer, "Thee should tremble at the word of the Lord." The officer laughed at the word "tremble" and called the followers of this sect "Quakers." The Puritans cut Quakers' ears, bored holes in their tongues, whipped them, and forced them out of town.*

d. Discuss the revolutionary reforms and ideas about freedom, criminal justice, and imprisonment Penn enacted in Pennsylvania's Constitution.

e. How did Penn seek to treat the Lenape and First Nations of Pennsylvania? What great rule guided him? *Penn strove to apply the Golden Rule to all dealings with the Lenape and Native Peoples.*

2. Choose an activity from the Crafts and Projects or Online Resources (pages 51-52) to enjoy with your student.

1. Seal of the State of Pennsylvania. 2. Statue of William Penn. 3. Statue of Tamanend.
4. *Penn's Treaty with the Indians at Shackamaxon* by Benjamin West, 1771.

LESSON 54

1. Have your student create a page in their notebook titled "William Penn Founds Pennsylvania, 1681." Have your student cut out the picture of William Penn, as well as the map of Pennsylvania, from the Picture Packet. Have your student color both and paste them in the notebook and record how Penn was granted the charter, as well as the meanings of Pennsylvania and Philadelphia (from page 36 of *The World of William Penn*).

2. Look at the painting titled *Penn's Treaty with the Indians at Shackamaxon* by Benjamin West (check out West's story in Rabbit Trails on page 51). Study the painting and then watch "The Making of an American Myth: Benjamin West, Penn's Treaty with the Indians," available at khanacademy.org. After viewing, consider how artistic works can shape public opinion. How does the painting make you feel? Now that you know that Thomas Penn (who commissioned the painting) did not honor the treaty his father established, do you feel differently about the painting? See if you can find the calumet in the picture. Do you remember what it symbolized?

3. The leader of the Lenni-Lenape was a man named Tamanend who was known as a lover of peace and friendship. Tamanend said the Lenape and the Quakers would "live in peace as long as the waters run in the rivers and creeks and as long as the stars and moon endure." These words have been memorialized on the statue of Tamanend pictured on the opposite page. Have your student write out the quote and draw a picture of Tamenend in the notebook.

LESSON 55

1. Read Chapter 6 of *A Child's First.* This reading will take us to the heart of the North American continent, where French missionaries and explorers were pressing into dense woods, crossing mountains, and navigating the mighty river called "Father of Waters" by the Anishinabe who lived along its shores. Discuss and contrast Marquette's approach to exploration with de Soto's.

2. Marquette and Joliet would have seen the Mound Builders' towering structures along the Mississippi. Learn more here: "Inside the Secret Mounds of Pre-Historic America" on the Ancient Mysteries YouTube channel.

LESSON 56

1. Read pages 53-70 of *The World of William Penn.* Take a moment to study the map on page 54 to familiarize the student with the main rivers and the Great Lakes.

> a. It had been nearly 200 years since Columbus discovered America, but explorers were still looking for a sea route to what continent? Why? *Explorers were still trying to find a sea route to Asia to access the rich spice and silk trade.*
>
> b. What was the calumet that the Illinois chief gave to Père Marquette? Why was it so important? What else did the chief send to the men, and why? *The calumet was a beautiful peace pipe of polished gray stone—a powerful symbol of peace between the Illinois that would be honored wherever they went. The chief also sent his son to demonstrate the love and friendship in his heart.*
>
> c. Why was La Salle's exploration of the length of the Mississippi important? What is the author showing by featuring the map on page 69? *La Salle was the first European to navigate the entire length of the Mississippi, and he felt entitled to claim the land for France. The author features the map to contrast how Europeans thought they had the right to claim what they "discovered" even though these lands had already been the homelands of Indigenous Peoples for thousands of years.*

2. Have your student draw a copy of the calumet seen on page 62 of *The World of William Penn.* Color it and paste it in the notebook along with a description of its importance.

3. To learn a bit more about La Salle, watch "The Life of Robert de La Salle – A Lesson for Kids" on the J. Ro YouTube channel.

LESSON 57

1. We will skip pages 71-100. Read pages 101-122 of *The World of William Penn.*

a. When the plague forced school closures, what two discoveries did Isaac Newton make? Who published Newton's findings? *Isaac Newton discovered the gravitational forces that keep the solar system revolving in perfect balance around the sun. He also found the properties of light and the spectrum of colors—red, orange, yellow, green, blue, indigo, and violet—that comprise light. Edmund Halley published Newton's discoveries in the book* Principia.

b. What did Edmund Halley discover about comets that also proved Newton's theories? *Edmund Halley discovered that comets revolve around the sun, just like the planets. The difference with comets is that their path is so vast that they take decades to reappear again in our orbit.*

c. What did Anton Van Leeuwenhoek call the microscopic life he discovered? *He called them "wee beasties."*

2. The following videos provide more information on the fascinating discoveries and people linked to the Royal Society.

The Royal Observatory at Greenwich established the prime meridian and revolutionized sailing, navigation, geography, and exploration. Learn more here: www.rmg.co.uk/royal-observatory/history

The following video explains the significance of Greenwich Mean Time:
"Greenwich Mean Time Explained I Time Zones For Kids" on The Touring Teacher YouTube channel

Learn more about Edmund Halley: www.ovovideo.com/en/edmund-halley/

LESSON 58

1. Read pages 123-132 of *The World of William Penn.* Study the family tree of the Stuarts on page 124.

a. When King James II took the throne, he wanted to revert England from a Protestant to a Catholic country. When he told William Penn, "I believe all men ought to have the freedom of their consciences," how did he sabotage himself? How did this episode change Penn's life? *The king assumed he could change the country by issuing a "Declaration of Indulgence" to end discrimination against Catholics and other sects. Though he professed "freedom of conscience," when bishops defied his royal order, he hypocritically threw them into the Tower of London. This action resulted in a revolt against King James and the loss of his throne. William Penn's friendship with the king placed him under suspicion, so he was arrested and charged with treason.*

b. What was the "Glorious Revolution," and why is it important in English history? *The "Glorious Revolution" commemorates the day that Parliament forced William III and Mary II to sign a Bill of Rights that would ensure that the king could never overrule Parliament.*

c. Why was William Penn arrested, and how did he lose Pennsylvania? How did he regain it? *William Penn was arrested because he was friends with the deposed king, James II. Penn lost Pennsylvania because the pacifist Quaker colonists were unwilling to fight against the French, so the king took Pennsylvania back. Penn was able to regain it by promising to pay the king money to protect it from the French.*

2. Earlier we learned about the differences between the northern and southern English colonies. Now that we are more familiar with Pennsylvania's history, you may enjoy watching "The Middle Colonies" at khanacademy.org.

LESSON 59

1. We will skip pages 133-178. Read pages 179-188 of *The World of William Penn.*

    a. What were William Penn's most challenging tasks in running the colony? What grand plan did Penn devise to help all the colonies? *Penn's most demanding tasks included mediating between Quakers and non-Quakers in the colony and capturing and punishing the pirates ravaging British shipping along the coast. Penn rightly foresaw that the colonies would do much better uniting together, and he called on them to join him and drafted a charter to this purpose.*

    b. Why did Penn return to England? *England was in another war initiated by Louis XIV; therefore, the colonies were also at war with France. Because Quakers are pacifists, Penn was obligated to contribute vast sums to the war effort or lose the colony. Simultaneously, someone sent negative reports to the Privy Council about Penn, undermining his position.*

    c. When the Lenape came to say goodbye to their friend "Brother Onus," how did the chieftain demonstrate the tribe's loyalty to the treaty? *The chieftain struck his hand to his head once and his heart three times, showing that "true covenants were made not with the head but with the heart."*

    d. The last years of William Penn's life were not easy. Why? *Penn was plagued by many financial worries, due to his dishonest secretary who had been cheating Penn for years. Penn was so deeply in debt that Hannah and their five children had to live with Hannah's father for some time. Then, when they were finally in their own home, Penn suffered a debilitating stroke.*

2. Have your student cut out, color, and paste the William Penn picture onto the timeline.

3. Conclude your study of William Penn by summarizing the key accomplishments of his life. Be sure to include how he was the first to establish the freedom of religion and speech, the right to a fair trial, and criminal justice reform in the colonies (see page 50 of *The World of William Penn*).

LESSON 60

1. Our study of the colonies began in Virginia, moved up to New England, and circled down to Pennsylvania. As we've progressed through the geographic regions of the thirteen colonies, we have also moved forward in time, and the North American continent looks much different than it did when Pocahontas and John Smith were forging ties between their distinct worlds. Learn more about how the colonies were changing and developing a unique identity apart from England. Watch "Developing an American Colonial Identity" on khanacademy.org.

2. A distinct aspect of colonial life during this period was the exploitation of enslaved people. Africans were kidnapped and sold as slaves; their unpaid labor bolstered the colonies' economic success. To incorporate this crucial facet of Colonial America into our study, we will read *Amos Fortune, Free Man*, the true story of a young African kidnapped and sold into slavery in 1725. Introduce *Amos Fortune* by Elizabeth Yates and read pages 3-13.

    a. How old was At-mun when he was kidnapped? *At-mun was 15 when slave traders abducted him.*

LESSON 61

1. Read pages 14-33 of *Amos Fortune.*

    a. Discuss the slave trade and what it meant for young At-mun.

2. Learn more about the slave trade and Middle Passage here: https://kids.kiddle.co/Middle_Passage

3. Choose an activity from the Crafts and Projects or Online Resources (pages 51-52) to do with your student.

The Atlantic Trade Triangle

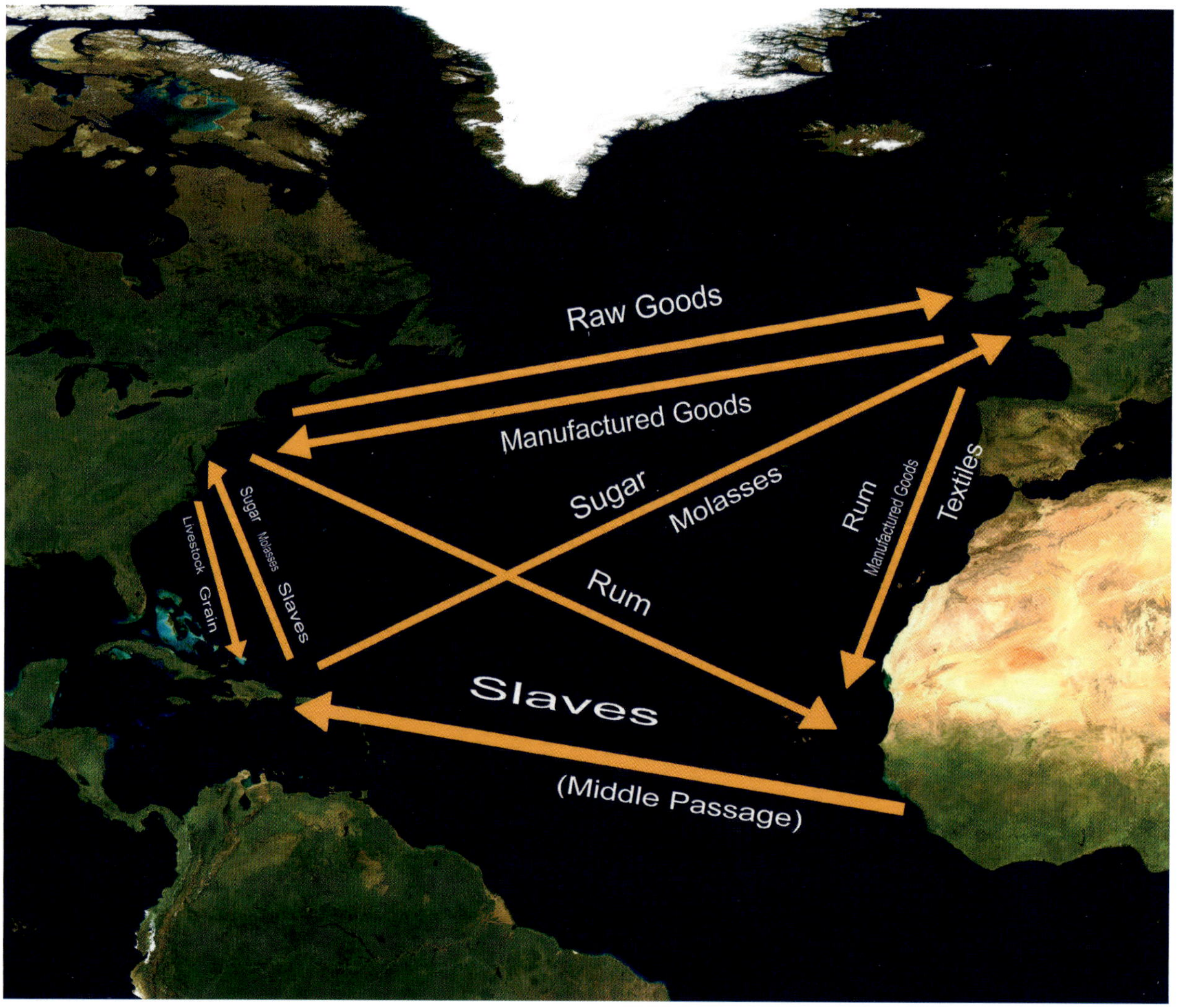

LESSON 62

1. Read pages 34-52 of *Amos Fortune.*

   a. Amos's friends call him Fortune. Why? *Amos's friends gave him the nickname Mr. Fortunatus as he had the good fortune of being bought by a family who did not mistreat him.*

   b. The Copelands were Quakers and, in principle, against slavery. Discuss the reasons Mr. Copeland felt compelled to purchase At-mun. How does Mr. Copeland justify himself? How do you think he could have been more just to Amos? Discuss if humane treatment is ever an adequate justification for slavery. In light of how slaveholders justified their right to the labor of those who served them without wages, see Lev. 19:13 and James 5:4.

   c. How did the Copeland family help educate Amos? *Unlike most slaveholders, the Copelands taught Amos to read, instructed him in the Bible, and included him in Quaker Meetings.*

   d. Discuss the difficulties Amos's enslaved friends faced and how their stories made him cautious about accepting manumission.

2. Have your student cut out the Middle Passage map in the Picture Packet and paste it into the notebook. Have your student write a paragraph explaining what the Middle Passage was and how people and goods were bought and sold in Europe, Africa, and the Americas.

LESSON 63

1. Read pages 53-80 of *Amos Fortune.*

   a. What political event took place the same year as the Boston Tea Party? *In 1773, a group of Blacks from Boston petitioned the legislature to ban the separation of families sold into slavery.*

   b. Contrast the African struggle for freedom with the American colonists' struggle against England. *Africans in the colonies struggled for the freedom of self-determination—the right to decide what they would do with their lives. The colonists were self-determined but lacked political representation, something Black Americans would not gain for 100 years. Blacks were regarded as property to be bought and sold. Colonists did not consider themselves truly "free" while they were subject to the whims of the British government.*

   c. The trade that Amos learned was tanning, and it was one of the most physically demanding of all vocations during the colonial period. Still, it could provide a comfortable life for the tanner. Learn more at the following website and even see a tanner's record book!
   www.colonialsense.com/Society-Lifestyle/Signs_of_the_Times/Tanning.php

   d. Discuss the conversation between Mr. and Mrs. Richardson on pages 63-64. How does Mr. Richardson's understanding of freedom differ from Amos's? Is it fair that he compared Amos's enslaved state to his own life as an unrepresented English subject?

   e. As the Revolutionary War was raging, Amos, too old for service, waged a war of his own. What was it? *He determined to buy the freedom of as many enslaved people as he was able.*

2. While Amos Fortune was making his way in Boston and suffering the disappointments that come with even the best of enslaved situations, the Indigenous tribes and nations increasingly felt the pressures of colonial encroachment on their lands. This led to multiple wars, the most decisive being the French and Indian War, fought for nine years beginning in 1754. Read Chapters 7 and 8 of *A Child's First.*

3. Have your student cut out the map titled "French and Indian War" in the Picture Packet and paste it into the notebook.

French & Indian War Resources

The French and Indian War raged during Amos Fortune's lifetime and set the stage for the Revolutionary War. To learn more about how this war took George Washington from obscurity to fame, created ties between the colonies and France, and eventually led to the taxes that would cause so much colonial unrest, check out the following links.

The Khan Academy has two videos explaining both the background and consequences of this first world war. Access them at khanacademy.org: "The Seven Years' War: background and combatants" and "The Seven Years' War: battles and legacy".

The following video provides further information on the French and Indian War: www.history.com/topics/native-american-history/french-and-indian-war-video

Learn more about George Washington's role in this war here: www.mountvernon.org/library/digitalhistory/digital-encyclopedia/article/french-and-indian-war/

Map of French and Indian War movements

LESSON 64

1. Read pages 81-108 of *Amos Fortune.*

2. Have your student cut out the map of the 13 colonies from the Picture Packet and paste it into the notebook.

LESSON 65

1. Read pages 109-129 of *Amos Fortune.*

2. Amos Fortune lived through the founding of the United States, and his life parallels the period of Benjamin Franklin's life. We will be studying the Revolutionary War in-depth in the next section, but for now, let's meet one of the most beloved of the founding fathers. Read Chapter 9 of *A Child's First.*

a. Benjamin Franklin expressed a wish to return 100 years after his death to see what the future would be. It has now been over 200 years since Franklin's death. Imagine what he would think of the world today. As an innovator and inventor, what do you think he would find astonishing, useful, and fantastic? What do you think might shock or disappoint him?

LESSON 66

1. Read pages 130-145 of *Amos Fortune.*

a. Why did Violet hide the iron kettle? How did Amos decide what to do with the money? *Violet did not want Amos to spend his hard-earned money on a woman who let herself be overcome with sorrow and shiftlessness. Amos climbed Mount Monadnock and sought the Lord's guidance. His heart was torn between helping Lois and buying land. Looking down from the mountain, he saw people going about their business working the land they owned; he realized that he had to take care of his family first; by purchasing land, he ensured their future.*

2. Read about Amos Fortune's continued legacy in the following article:
www.latimes.com/archives/la-xpm-1988-11-13-vw-237-story.html

LESSON 67

1. Finish reading *Amos Fortune* over the next couple of days.

a. Explain "vendue" and discuss this colonial practice. How was this a way for a community to care for the needy and helpless? *"Vendue" was a system devised in pioneer towns to enable the town to care for the poor. Townsfolk could bid at auctions to provide care for an indigent person for a year. See page 152.*

b. Discuss "My hand was restrained and I'm glad that it was, for the years between have shown me that it does a man no good to be free until he knows how to live, how to walk in-step with God."

c. Why did Amos donate money to his church and the local school? *Amos left his money to the local church and school because they had been vital to his life and development as a man of God.*

d. Have your student narrate Amos Fortune's life and describe three character traits that he or she finds particularly admirable in this great man.

2. During Amos Fortune's lifetime, attitudes toward slavery were shifting, setting the stage for a future civil war. Learn more by watching "Regional attitudes about slavery, 1754-1800" at khanacademy.org.

3. Read Chapter 10 of *A Child's First.*

Historic Table

Colonial Tea Party

To celebrate the conclusion of your colonial studies, plan a tea party with delights both savory and sweet that would have been common entrées on a tea table in the 1700s. The selections featured opposite are shrimp salad sandwiches, mini blinis with herbed cream cheese, lemon poppy seed scones with Devonshire cream and lemon curd, old-fashioned strawberry shortcakes, and mini lemon tartes.

One of the most common teas favored by New Englanders was Bohea tea. This smoky flavored tea will bring an authentic flair to your party. It was Bohea tea that Patriots threw into Boston Harbor protesting the British tax on tea. For those who prefer a Liberty tea—the herbal teas made in protest to English tea—look at bostonteapartyship.com for many ideas. Bohea tea is available online.

Shrimp Salad Sandwiches

1 pound shrimp cooked, cleaned, and shelled, chopped
1/3 cup mayonnaise
1/2 cup celery, finely chopped
1 green onion, finely chopped
1 teaspoon Old Bay seasoning
1 teaspoon fresh dill, chopped
Mustard greens or baby arugula to garnish
White bread with crusts removed
Salt and pepper to taste

Mix all ingredients. Lightly toast white bread, fill with shrimp salad, top with greens, cut in triangles, and serve well chilled.

Herbed Cream Cheese Blinis

1 package mini blinis
1 8-ounce package cream cheese
Thinly sliced radishes
Thinly sliced cucumbers
Seasoned salt
Fresh dill, basil, chives, parsley (about 2 tablespoons each chopped and mixed)

Allow cream cheese to warm slightly. Then press into a log shape and roll in fresh herbs, coating the outside. Sprinkle with seasoned salt and pepper. Refrigerate while slicing cucumbers and radishes. Slice cream cheese log into rounds. Layer blinis with cucumbers, cream cheese, and radishes. Serve well chilled.

Lemon Poppy Seed Scones

Follow the Amazing Lemon Scones recipe on allrecipes.com. This recipe is a healthy option if you omit the sugar glaze. Add 2 full tablespoons of lemon zest and 2 tablespoons of poppy seeds. You can eliminate the glaze, as these scones are served with lemon curd and Devonshire cream—both are available at World Market or gourmet groceries.

Old-Fashioned Strawberry Shortcake

Follow sallysbakingaddiction.com directions for light, fluffy, and flakey biscuits. Slice and sweeten strawberries to taste. Chill. Whip organic whipping cream with 1-2 tablespoons confectioner's sugar and 1 teaspoon vanilla extract. When the biscuits are baked, slice each in half. Butter the bottom half and layer with strawberries and whipped cream. Top with biscuit half.

Mini Lemon Tartes

Follow the recipe for shortbread crust on bakerbettie.com. If available, press mixture into mini tarte pans. After baking, let tartes cool and then fill with desired sweets—raspberry jam, lemon curd, lingonberry jam, or even apple butter. Top with a dollop of whipped cream. Serve well chilled.

"There is a great deal of poetry and fine sentiment in a cup of tea."

— Ralph Waldo Emerson

The Battle of Long Island by Dominick D'Andrea

The Revolutionary War

England had a problem. Their colonists were increasingly restless and had begun refusing to obey the demands of the crown. What to do? The colonists had a problem too. They were losing their identity as English citizens and beginning to think of themselves more as New Yorkers, Bostonians, Rhode Islanders, Virginians, and Pennsylvanians. The mother country was a long way off, and she was becoming more and more demanding. An expensive war against the French and their Indian allies had cost colonists' lives, and now Britain was demanding that they pay higher taxes to pay for this war. But were the colonists represented in Parliament—the government body—legislating these taxes? No.

The colonists, subjects of a government in which they had no voice, looked around at the cities and towns they had built and started to question what they owed the crown. The seeds of independence were sown. Over time these seeds would sprout, and a bloody eight-year war would ensue, and a new nation would emerge. This new nation had a historically unique opportunity to define itself, to establish a government that derived its power from the people. But the process of uniting and creating this new government required passionate debate, conviction, and ultimately, compromise. What came from years of arguing was "a more perfect union." This new form of representative government was a triumph of fiercely held convictions as well as deep compromise. The freedoms extended to those considered citizens included free speech, free exercise of religion, and a free press—each one enshrined in a brilliant, though intensely debated, Bill of Rights. The separation of powers and checks and balances were ingeniously crafted. It indeed was "more perfect." But, because flawed humans built it, it could never be entirely perfect.

While the idea of freedom was held high, it was also denied to the hundreds of thousands of Black enslaved people whose unrequited labor helped build the wealth and status of this nation. Indeed, many Blacks even fought in the Revolution. Voting rights were reserved for white male landowners, effectively silencing the majority of Americans' voices. The United States, a beacon of freedom and hope to the world, was just beginning her journey to grow into a country that genuinely embodies her highest ideals. This process continues to this day as we debate, listen, vote, and participate in the ongoing process of shaping our country.

Rabbit Trails

Eliza: The Story of Elizabeth Schuyler Hamilton by Margaret McNamara
The story of Alexander Hamilton's extraordinary wife. She not only helped further her husband's career, but after his death she became an activist, philanthropist, and curator of Alexander's legacy in America's founding.

Henry Knox: Bookseller, Soldier, Patriot by Anita Silvey
The story of one of America's most unlikely but lovable patriots. Knox did not look heroic, but his actions were directly responsible for helping America win the war for independence.

The Escape of Oney Judge by Emily Arnold McCulley
Tells the true story of Martha Washington's personal slave girl and how she escaped bondage at age 17 to live her life as a free woman.

Revolutionary Friends: General George Washington and the Marquis de Lafayette by Selene Castrovilla
The warm and tender story of Lafayette's devotion to Washington and to the cause of freedom in America.

A Spy Called James: The True Story of James Lafayette by Anne Rockwell
The tale of a true hero of the Revolution, who acted as spy gathering critical information. His service should have earned him his freedom, but it did not. That was another battle he must fight.

Thomas Jefferson: Life, Liberty, and the Pursuit of Everything by Maira Kalman
Tells the story of one of America's most contradictory and influential founders.

Worst of Friends: Thomas Jefferson and John Adams by Suzanne Tripp Jurmain
Two men could not be more different, and yet together Adams and Jefferson helped create one of the most enduring democracies in history. But when their friendship breaks down, it takes decades for it to repair.

Crafts & Projects

The Revolutionary War

Visit the link below and click on the various sections to learn more about different aspects of the Revolution and War for Independence:
www.dkfindout.com/us/history/american-revolution/

Pretend to Be a Spy

As you read *Toliver's Secret*, you will learn about the spy networks used to send messages during the Revolutionary War. These messages were mostly written in code. Using the activities at the link below, learn how to write coded letters and decode secret messages. Try this over the next two lessons as you read about Ellen's adventure.
www.historyisfun.org/wp-content/uploads/2015/12/I-Spy-Worksheets-web.pdf

Train Like a Patriot

Baron von Steuben was a key figure in raising morale among the Continental soldiers. His expertise and ability to train soldiers were vital in turning them into effective fighters. Learn (and practice!) his drills.
www.historyisfun.org/wp-content/uploads/2014/05/AnnasAdventures_DrillingCommands_v3.pdf

Brush Up on Military Lingo

For an excellent explanation and drawings of redoubts, check out the site below:
www.revolutionarywarjournal.com/redoubts

George Washington, Spymaster
by Thomas B. Allen

Black Heroes of the American Revolution
by Burke Davis

Ben and Me by Robert Lawson

Traitor: The Case of Benedict Arnold and *Alexander Hamilton: The Outsider*
by Jean Fritz

The Duel: The Parallel Lives of Alexander Hamilton and Aaron Burr
by Judith St. George

Online Resources

Liberty! The American Revolution: www.pbs.org/ktca/liberty/teachers.html

George Washington's Mount Vernon: www.mountvernon.org/

Character Connection: Self-Control

The colonists were growing more anxious for independence from England. This movement was driven by the colonists' belief that Britain was abusing its power as their government and colonists wanted to be self-governing. This idea had deep roots in North America. We saw this in the Five Nations Confederacy and the Pilgrims' Mayflower Compact. As the cry for freedom mounted, there was widespread recognition that in order to be free and independent from England, the colonists must exercise self-control. Use the following verses and proverbs to prompt character discussion.

Proverbs 13:3
Proverbs 16:32
Proverbs 18:6-7
Proverbs 25:27-28
Proverbs 29:11

Matthew 5:29-30
1 Corinthians 9:24-27
Galatians 5:22-23
Philippians 4:11-13
1 Thessalonians 4:3-4

1 Timothy 2-3
2 Timothy 3:1-5
Titus 2:6-12
James 1:19

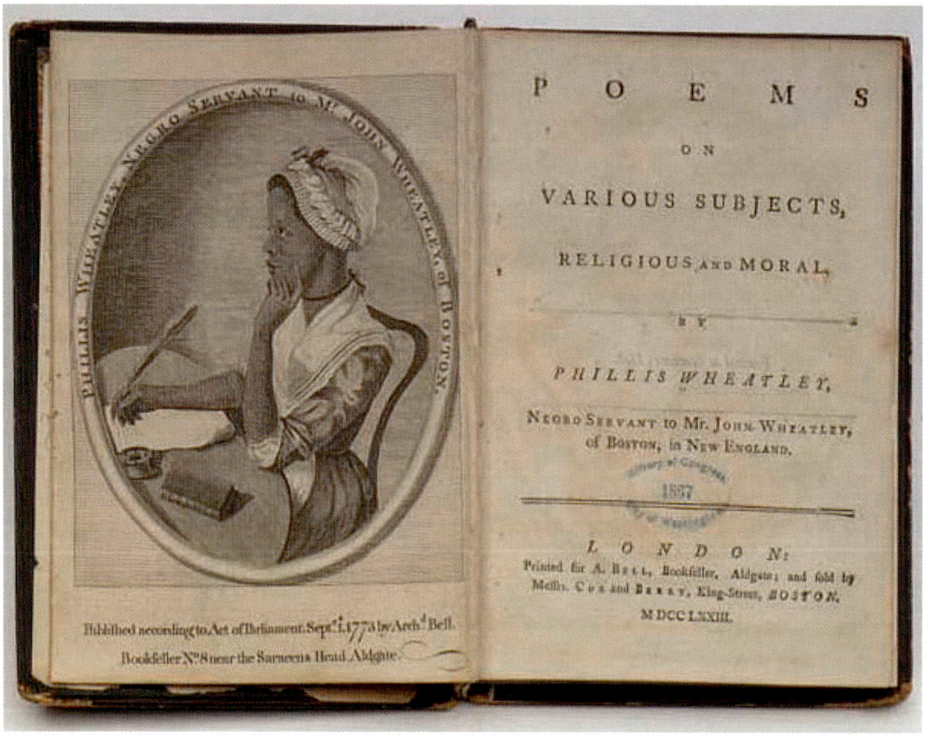

1. *Poems on Various Subjects, Religious and Moral* by Phillis Wheatley, engraving attributed to Scipio Moorhead, 1773. 2. Abolitionist woodcarvings used by the Society for the Abolition of Slavery in England.

LESSON 68

1. Phillis Wheatley's life spanned a period of tremendous change in the colonies as they became more independent and frustrated with England. Wheatley's poetry provides a unique lens through which we can view this tumultuous and triumphant period of history. Introduce *A Voice of Her Own: The Story of Phillis Wheatley, Slave Poet* by Kathryn Lasky. Read Chapters 1-3. In place of comprehension and discussion questions, each lesson for this section includes a selection of Wheatley's poems and writings. Analysis and commentary are provided for select poems.

2. Read Phillis's first two published poems and watch the following videos for analysis and explanation of "On Being Brought from Africa to America."

"On Being Brought from Africa to America"
by Phillis Wheatley

'Twas mercy brought me from my Pagan land,
Taught my benighted soul to understand
That there's a God, that there's a Saviour too:
Once I redemption neither sought nor knew.
Some view our sable race with scornful eye,
"Their colour is a diabolic die."
Remember, Christians, Negros, black as Cain,
May be refin'd, and join th' angelic train.

Watch:

"Phillis Wheatley's 'On Being Brought from Africa to America' Read by Cornelius Eady" on the Tate Street YouTube Channel

"Analyzing Phillis Wheatley's 'On Being Brought From Africa to America'" on the Tammie Pierce YouTube Channel

Read Phillis Wheatley's first published poem in the *Newport Mercury*, December 21, 1767, introduced as follows:

To The Printer:
Please to insert the following Lines, composed by a Negro Girl (belonging to one Mr. Wheatley of Boston) on the following Occasion, viz. Messrs Hussey and Coffin, as undermentioned, belonging to Nantucket, being bound from thence to Boston, narrowly escaped being cast away on Cape-Cod, in one of the late Storms; upon their Arrival, being at Mr. Wheatley's, and, while at Dinner, told of their narrow Escape, this Negro Girl at the same Time 'tending Table, heard the Relation, from which she composed the following Verses.

Did Fear and Danger so perplex your Mind,
As made you fearful of the Whistling Wind?
Was it not Boreas knit his angry Brow
Against you? or did Consideration bow?
To lend you Aid, did not his Winds combine?
To stop your passage with a churlish Line,
Did haughty Eolus with Contempt look down
With Aspect windy, and a study'd Frown?
Regard them not; — the Great Supreme, the Wise,
Intends for something hidden from our Eyes.
Suppose the groundless Gulph had snatch'd away
Hussey and Coffin to the raging Sea;
Where wou'd they go? where wou'd be their Abode?
With the supreme and independent God,
Or made their Beds down in the Shades below,
Where neither Pleasure nor Content can flow.
To Heaven their Souls with eager Raptures soar,
Enjoy the Bliss of him they wou'd adore.
Had the soft gliding Streams of Grace been near,
Some favourite Hope their fainting hearts to cheer,
Doubtless the Fear of Danger far had fled:
No more repeated Victory crown their Heads.

Had I the Tongue of a Seraphim, how would I exalt thy Praise; thy Name as Incense to the Heavens should fly, and the Remembrance of thy Goodness to the shoreless Ocean of Beatitude! — Then should the Earth glow with seraphick Ardour. Blest Soul, which sees the Day while Light doth shine, To guide his Steps to trace the Mark divine.

LESSON 69

1. Read Chapters 4-5 of *A Voice of Her Own.*

2. Read and discuss Wheatley's poem "On Imagination."

"On Imagination"
by Phillis Wheatley

THY various works, imperial queen, we see,
How bright their forms! how deck'd with pomp by thee!
Thy wondrous acts in beauteous order stand,
And all attest how potent is thine hand.

Imagination! who can sing thy force?
Or who describe the swiftness of thy course?
Soaring through air to find the bright abode,
Th' empyreal palace of the thund'ring God,
We on thy pinions can surpass the wind,
And leave the rolling universe behind:

From star to star the mental optics rove,
Measure the skies, and range the realms above.
There in one view we grasp the mighty whole
Or with new worlds amaze th' unbounded soul.

3. Crispus Attucks, one of the first Americans to die in the Revolutionary War, was a formerly enslaved Black man. Learn more here: www.biography.com/military-figure/crispus-attucks

Watch a celebration of Crispus Attucks: "A Tribute to Crispus Attucks – Part 1" on the AAHPC YouTube channel.

4. Have your student cut out, color, and paste the Boston Massacre picture onto the timeline.

LESSON 70

1. Finish reading *A Voice of Her Own.*

2. Read and discuss the following excerpt from a letter Wheatley wrote to Reverend Samson Occom:

"Otherwise, perhaps, the Israelites had been less solicitous for their Freedom from Egyptian Slavery: I don't say they would have been contented without it, by no Means, for in every human Breast, God has implanted a Principle, which we call Love of freedom; it is impatient of Oppression, and pants for Deliverance; and by the Leave of our modern Egyptians, I will assert that the same Principle lives in us." Letter to Reverend Samson Occom and published in Boston newspapers in 1774.

3. Read and discuss Wheatley's poem on George Washington. You will see that Wheatley's legacy lives on in the name of our nation's capital, Washington, District of Columbia. Wheatley personifies the United States as a classical goddess she calls Columbia. This image entered the American imagination quickly, and when the leaders were debating names for the capital district, they selected Columbia.

"His Excellency General Washington"
by Phillis Wheatley

Celestial choir! enthron'd in realms of light,
Columbia's scenes of glorious toils I write.
While freedom's cause her anxious breast alarms,
She flashes dreadful in refulgent arms.
See mother earth her offspring's fate bemoan,
And nations gaze at scenes before unknown!
See the bright beams of heaven's revolving light
Involved in sorrows and the veil of night!

The Goddess comes, she moves divinely fair,
Olive and laurel binds Her golden hair:
Wherever shines this native of the skies,
Unnumber'd charms and recent graces rise.

Muse! Bow propitious while my pen relates
How pour her armies through a thousand gates,
As when Eolus heaven's fair face deforms,
Enwrapp'd in tempest and a night of storms;
Astonish'd ocean feels the wild uproar,
The refluent surges beat the sounding shore;
Or think as leaves in Autumn's golden reign,
Such, and so many, moves the warrior's train.

In bright array they seek the work of war,
Where high unfurl'd the ensign waves in air.
Shall I to Washington their praise recite?
Enough thou know'st them in the fields of fight.
Thee, first in peace and honors—we demand
The grace and glory of thy martial band.
Fam'd for thy valour, for thy virtues more,
Hear every tongue thy guardian aid implore!

One century scarce perform'd its destined round,
When Gallic powers Columbia's fury found;
And so may you, whoever dares disgrace
The land of freedom's heaven-defended race!
Fix'd are the eyes of nations on the scales,
For in their hopes Columbia's arm prevails.
Anon Britannia droops the pensive head,
While round increase the rising hills of dead.
Ah! Cruel blindness to Columbia's state!
Lament thy thirst of boundless power too late.

Proceed, great chief, with virtue on thy side,
Thy ev'ry action let the Goddess guide.
A crown, a mansion, and a throne that shine,
With gold unfading, WASHINGTON! Be thine.

For analysis, visit: www.encyclopedia.com/arts/educational-magazines/his-excellency-general-washington

LESSON 71

1. Have your student cut out and color Phillis Wheatley's picture and paste it on the timeline. Have your student conclude this section on Wheatley by writing out their favorite Wheatley poem in the notebook.

2. As we read in *A Voice of Her Own*, the colonists were growing increasingly weary of being governed by what many were beginning to see as a distant and demanding government. We will now explore the American Revolution. This section involves a bit of jumping around both in chronology and book selections. We will be reading from multiple books to give an accurate understanding of this period's complexities. Introduce *George vs. George: The American Revolution as Seen from Both Sides* by Rosalyn Schanzer. Read pages 7-17.

   a. Page 15 makes a note of Britain's official position on colonial settlement. Read more about the Proclamation Line of 1763 here: www.historyisfun.org/learn/learning-center/what-was-the-proclamation-of-1763/

   b. Compare the systems of government pictured on pages 16 and 17. What differences stand out to you? Can you identify structures of the English system that the colonists would want to reject?

LESSON 72

1. Read pages 18-22 of *George vs. George.*

   a. Watch "Sons of Liberty History" on The Daily Bellringer YouTube channel to learn more about this revolutionary group.

   b. Discuss the merits of both the Colonial and English positions.

2. Have your student cut out, color, and paste the Boston Tea Party picture onto the timeline.

LESSON 73

1. Read pages 23-25 of *George v. George.*

2. Read about why the colonists chose to dress up as Mohawks here: www.bostonteapartyship.com/disguise-of-sons-of-liberty

3. Read Chapter 11 of *A Child's First.*

   a. Discuss the difference between an act of rebellion and an act of theft. Read more about the rules governing the Boston Tea Party here: https://mrnussbaum.com/rules-of-the-boston-tea-party

LESSON 74

1. Read Chapter 12 of *A Child's First.* The colonies are now at war with England!

2. Read pages 26-31 of *George vs. George.*

3. Mark the following Massachusetts landmarks on the map of the colonies in the notebook:

Boston	Lexington	Concord
Bunker Hill	Breed's Hill	

4. Have your student cut out, color, and paste the Paul Revere's Ride picture onto the timeline.

LESSON 75

1. It is easy to assume that if you lived at the time of the American Revolution, you would have picked the colonies' side. Watch the following video to see the other options that may have been open to you: "Would You Have Joined the American Revolution?" on the Origin of Everything YouTube channel.

2. Read pages 32-35 of *George vs. George*.

   a. Discuss the differences between the British and Rebel forces.

3. Have your student cut out the images of British and Colonial Soldiers in the Picture Packet. Color, label, and add them to the notebook.

LESSON 76

1. Read Chapter 13 of *A Child's First*.

2. In addition to declaring independence from Britain, the Continental Congress drew up the Articles of Confederation. Learn more about the precursor to the United States Constitution by watching the following: "The Articles of Confederation - The Constitution Before the Constitution" on the Today I Found Out YouTube channel.

3. Read pages 36-37 of *George vs. George*.

   a. On page 90 of this guide, you can see a painting that reimagines the destruction of King George's statue by colonial rebels. Discuss this act of rebellion and protest. There is an ongoing debate about the destruction of monuments to Confederate soldiers and generals in the U.S. today. Some want them removed, and others argue that they represent our nation's history. How does the historical precedent represented in this painting affect your view of these current events?

4. Have your student cut out, color, and paste the Declaration of Independence picture onto the timeline.

LESSON 77

1. Read the text of the Declaration of Independence at the National Archives: www.archives.gov/founding-docs/declaration-transcript

   a. Discuss the following concepts presented in the preamble:
      - the right to rebel against tyrannical governments
      - self-evident rights
      - rights to life, liberty, and the pursuit of happiness
      - governmental power is from the consent of the people
      - the government should not be changed for "light and transient causes"

   b. Which of King George's listed grievances stands out to you? Why?

2. Have your student write out the preamble to the Declaration of Independence in the notebook. Add the Continental Congress illustration from the Picture Packet to the notebook.

3. Have your student mark the following important Revolutionary War landmarks on the map in the notebook:

Green Mountains	Ticonderoga	Crown Point
Valley Forge	Vincennes	Trenton, NJ
Delaware River	New York City	Elizabeth, NJ

The Boston Tea Party by John Andrews, 1856

LESSON 78

1. During the Revolutionary War, rebel colonists found themselves doing things they would have never imagined as loyal British subjects. Our next book is about a girl who accepts a secret mission to support the rebel cause. While this book is not the story of an actual person, it captures the many roles that colonists, including children, played during the rebellion. It also helps readers understand the costs of war, how it affected the colonies, and what life was like during this pivotal moment in U.S. history. Introduce *Toliver's Secret* by Esther Wood Brady. Read Chapters 1-2.

   a. The British government forced colonists to house and feed British soldiers in the colonists' homes! Discuss how this affects Ellen's family. How would it feel to be forced to allow enemy soldiers to live in your house?

   b. Ellen and her family, being rebel colonists, must be very careful about what they say in New York City. Why? *Most of the residents of NYC remained loyal to the British.*

   c. Describe Ellen. What characteristics would you use to explain her personality to someone?

LESSON 79

1. Read Chapters 3-5 of *Toliver's Secret.*

   a. Discuss Grandfather's statement: "We get over fear by doing things we think we cannot do." Can you think of a time in your life when you found this to be true?

2. Ellen runs into part of New York City that has burned down. Read more about this fire at the following sites:
   https://virtualny.ashp.cuny.edu/FIRE/greatfire1776.html
   www.dkfindout.com/us/history/american-revolution/great-fire-new-york-1776/

3. Choose an activity from the Crafts and Projects or Online Resources (page 79) to enjoy with your student.

LESSON 80

1. Read Chapters 6-8 of *Toliver's Secret.*

2. Continue working on your craft or project.

Boston Massacre by Paul Revere, based on earlier engraving by Harry Pelham, 1770

LESSON 81

1. Read Chapters 9-10 of *Toliver's Secret.*

    a. War always displaces people and creates refugee populations, and the Revolutionary War was no different. Ellen remembers passing refugees when she walks to New York City with her mother. These people had lost their homes in the battle between the patriots and the English or the subsequent fire. In a way, Ellen and her mother were refugees too. They sought a new home because of the war's effect on their lives. They were fortunate enough to have a relative who could accommodate them, but many war refugees throughout history have not been so lucky. Discuss how war creates these vulnerable populations. Look through news articles to learn more about the refugee crises today. Wars in the Middle East, drug wars in Central and South America, and other conflicts have created an unprecedented refugee crisis.

2. Using Grandfather as inspiration, discuss with your student how you could go about smuggling secret messages to a friend or relative.

LESSON 82

1. Finish reading *Toliver's Secret.*

    a. What battle did Ellen help George Washington win? *The Battle at Trenton.*

    b. Discuss how Ellen overcame obstacle after obstacle. List the challenges Ellen faced on her journey. How does each event change Ellen? *Every time Ellen faced one of her fears or overcame a challenge, she was able to look back on it and realize that she was stronger, braver, quicker, and fiercer than she ever imagined.*

    c. How did Grandfather's words at the beginning of the story about facing fears play out? *As Ellen faced different fears, she became braver, and that courage grew over her day-long adventure.*

    d. Ellen draws strength from Isaiah 40. Read this aloud, and have your student write their favorite verses in the notebook.

2. To visualize Elizabeth's journey, look at an online map of New York and New Jersey. Search for Front Street, NYC. You will find it at the southernmost end of Manhattan. On Google Maps, you will be able to see Fraunces' Tavern, an important meeting place for patriots during the British occupation of New York City, nearby. It was probably this tavern that Grandfather visited when he twisted his ankle. Once you have located these landmarks, zoom out to see Elizabeth, NJ, and Perth Amboy, NJ. What do you think of Ellen's journey now?

3. Read pages 38-43 of *George vs. George.*

    a. George Washington's victory at Trenton is memorialized in one of U.S. history's most well-known paintings. Look up *Washington Crossing the Delaware* by Emanuel Leutze on the internet. Do you think this is a historically accurate portrayal of how Washington crossed the Delaware River with his soldiers?

4. Have your student cut out the American Revolutionary War map from the Picture Packet and add it to the notebook.

1. *Advance of the Enemy* by Alfred Wordsworth Thompson.
2. *Pulling Down the Statue of King George III, New York City* by Johannes Adam Simon Oertel.

LESSON 83

1. Read Chapters 14 and 15 of *A Child's First.*

2. Read pages 44-47 of *George vs. George.*

   a. Valley Forge, at the time of the Continental Army's encampment there, was the fourth-largest city in the colonies! Read more here: www.nps.gov/vafo/learn/historyculture/valley-forge-history-and-significance.htm

3. If desired, watch "George Washington–The Founding Fathers & The American Revolution Documentary" on The Peoples Profiles YouTube channel.

LESSON 84

1. We are now going to learn about a critical figure in the American Revolutionary War, the Marquis de Lafayette. To introduce Lafayette to your student, watch "Liberty's Kids 122 - Lafayette Arrives" on YouTube.

2. Read Chapters 1-2 of *Why Not, Lafayette?* by Jean Fritz.

   a. What was Lafayette's full name, and what did his family call him? *Marie Joseph Paul Yves Roch Gilbert de Motier, Marquis de Lafayette. His family called him Gilbert (in French,* Zhil-Bear*).* How old were Lafayette and Adrienne when they married? *Lafayette was 16, and Adrienne was 14 years old.*

   b. Why was 1776 an important year for Lafayette? *It was the year the colonies declared their independence from England, and Lafayette wanted to support the revolution.*

   c. Once Lafayette decided to join the American patriots, he faced a tough challenge. What was it, and with whom did he share his secret plans? *Because Lafayette was so young, he had to ask permission of his father-in-law and the king. Because he knew they would not permit him, he made his plans in secret, telling only the American ambassadors—Silas Deane and Benjamin Franklin.*

   d. In Chapter 2, Lafayette made a very generous provision for his troops. What is it? *Lafayette outfitted his soldiers with uniforms and boots using his own money.* What happened in April 1778 that greatly encouraged Washington and Lafayette? *The French signed a treaty of alliance between the American patriots and France.*

3. To learn more about the battles in the Revolutionary War and Washington's role in leading his soldiers, watch "Washington's War" on the George Washington's Mount Vernon YouTube channel.

1. *Battle of Guilford Court House* by H. Charles McBarron.
2. *Marquis de Lafayette meets the National Guard in New York in 1825.*

LESSON 85

1. In preparation for the next reading, watch "Liberty's Kids 124 - Vally Forge" on YouTube.

2. Read Chapters 3-4 of *Why Not, Lafayette?*

   a. When Lafayette returned to France, what were his goals? *Lafayette wanted to find out the king's plans, to seek counsel regarding whether he should fight with the French or with the patriots, and to secure more supplies and money from France.*

   b. While Lafayette waited in Virginia, what important work did he send his valet Jim to do? If desired, watch "Liberty's Kids 135 - James Armistead."
   Jim was to pose as a runaway slave, cross into enemy territory, and discover the British plans.

   c. What courageous action did Alexander Hamilton take in the battle of Yorktown? *Hamilton bravely signaled a final redoubt, and fought the British in hand-to-hand combat, leading his men to victory.*

   d. After the American victory, how did Cornwallis snub Washington? *He didn't show up for the traditional surrendering of arms to hand over his sword to Washington. Instead, he sent his second-in-command, who gave the sword to Rochambeau. This was an intentional insult to Washington, indicating the French had won the war. But Rochambeau was a gentleman and, refusing the sword, nodded in the direction of Washington.*

3. Have your student write out Washington's parting words to Lafayette on page 33 of *Why Not, Lafayette?* and add them to the notebook.

LESSON 86

1. Watch "Liberty's Kids 136 - Yorktown"on YouTube.

2. Read Chapters 5-6 of *Why Not, Lafayette?*

   a. When Lafayette returned to France, there was one thing he wished he had. What was it? *Lafayette missed the American mockingbird.*

   b. What reforms did Lafayette begin in France? *He tried to end slavery in the French territories by buying two plantations with the intention of training and freeing the slaves.* What did Lafayette do when the people stormed the Bastille? *He ordered the infamous prison burned.*

   c. Why was Lafayette arrested? *As part of the aristocracy, he was seen by the radicals as an enemy of the people. Many aristocrats were guillotined.* In Chapter 6, when Lafayette was in prison, what extraordinary thing happened? *His wife, Adrienne, and their two daughters came to share his imprisonment.*

   d. When Napoleon's brother tried to rally the assembly leaders to continue supporting Napoleon's wars, what did Lafayette do? *He reproached the assembly, reminding them that three million Frenchmen had already laid down their lives in Napoleon's fruitless wars.*

3. Learn more about the distinctive mockingbird that Lafayette so admired. Cut out the northern mockingbird picture from the Picture Packet, and have your student add it to the notebook along with a few facts about these birds.

4. Choose an activity from the Crafts and Projects or Online Resources (page 79) to enjoy with your student.

LESSON 87

1. Read Chapters 7-8 of *Why Not, Lafayette?*

a. What impressed Lafayette when he visited Washington, D.C.? *The republican tone deeply moved him—there were no guards on duty, cabinet ministers often answered the door themselves. In a meeting with the president, there was no special chair for the chief executive; the president also dressed like everyone else. These things were unheard of in France.*

b. In Chapter 8, Lafayette experienced a new technology. What was it? *The steamboat.* What did Lafayette lose when the steamboat sank? *The 600 letters he was about to start answering.*

c. What important anniversary did Lafayette celebrate in Boston? *Lafayette laid the wreath to mark the fiftieth anniversary of the Battle of Bunker Hill and dedicate the monument there.*

d. What American delight did the people of Maine introduce to Lafayette? *Ice cream.*

e. Have the student record from page 67 the parting words of President John Quincy Adams to Lafayette.

2. In Chapter 7, Lafayette was invited to visit America in 1824 by President James Monroe. So beloved was Lafayette as a Revolutionary hero that the celebrations and honors he was given were unparalleled in American history. At Fort Lafayette, the West Point band played "See the Conquering Hero Comes!", a celebratory anthem written by G. F. Handel as part of his *Judas Maccabaeus* oratorio. Listen to a beautiful rendition of it by accessing "Judas Maccabaeus, HWV 63: See, the Conqu'ring Hero Comes!" on The Tabernacle Choir at Temple Square YouTube channel.

LESSON 88

1. Read Chapters 9-10 of *Why Not, Lafayette?*

a. What disappointments did Lafayette find on his return home? *King Charles had restored all the rights of the aristocracy that Lafayette had fought so hard to end. King Charles was defying the constitution, and he abolished the National Guard, which Lafayette had started.*

b. What did Lafayette realize about the fight for liberty in France? *Liberty could not be fought and won once and for all. It had to be fought for over and over.*

2. To conclude this study on the Marquis de Lafayette's life, watch "Washington's Generals Marquis de Lafayette" on the YouTube History Channel.

3. Have your student write a brief report on Lafayette's life, especially regarding his devotion to the American cause of liberty and his tireless work to bring freedom to France, including his work to eliminate slavery. Illustrate with drawings or pictures of Lafayette and add the report to the notebook.

LESSON 89

1. It is essential to recognize that revolutions, no matter how noble their ideals, are nearly always messy and violent, and they come at a great cost, setting neighbor against neighbor, dividing families, and resulting in loss of all kinds. The destruction inherent in a revolution is widespread. The American Revolution was an opportunity for great men and women to rise to the call of their emerging nation. Many did, exhibiting courage, self-sacrifice, and dedication to a cause greater than themselves. It also produced a sort of lawless frenzy that resulted in reckless and destructive actions on the part of some Revolutionaries and Tories. Read more about this on pages 48-49 of *George vs. George.*

2. Abigail Adams, wife of John Adams, like many women in her time, played an essential role in the Revolution. Introduce *Remember the Ladies: A Story about Abigail Adams* by Jeri Chase Ferris. This book will review some of the events leading up to the Revolutionary War, but it also provides a window into the domestic lives of women and children during this period. Read Chapters 1-3.

a. How did Abigail's father encourage her to pursue learning? *He told her that her fine mind was a gift from God.*

b. What was Abigail's position on slavery? *She saw the inconsistency in the colonists fighting for freedom while they were "daily robbing . . . from those who have as good a right to freedom as we have."*

c. Which of Abigail's sacrifices for the cause of independence stands out most to you? Discuss.

3. Watch "Articles of Confederation" on khanacademy.org.

LESSON 90

1. Read Chapters 4-6 of *Remember the Ladies.*

a. Define *duty*. Discuss this concept and the Adams' mutual commitment to fulfilling what they saw as their duty to their country. Reflect on your obligations, discuss how you feel about duty, how you fulfill your responsibilities, and how you may fail at times.

2. Read about Abigail Adams's experience in inoculating her family against smallpox in July 1776:
www.washingtonpost.com/history/2020/12/12/abigail-adams-smallpox-coronavirus-vaccine/

3. It was some time in 1776 or 1777 that the first flag representing the new American republic was designed. Watch the following documentary to learn more about this important national symbol: "National Constitution Center 'The History of the U.S. Flag'" on the National Constitution Center YouTube channel.

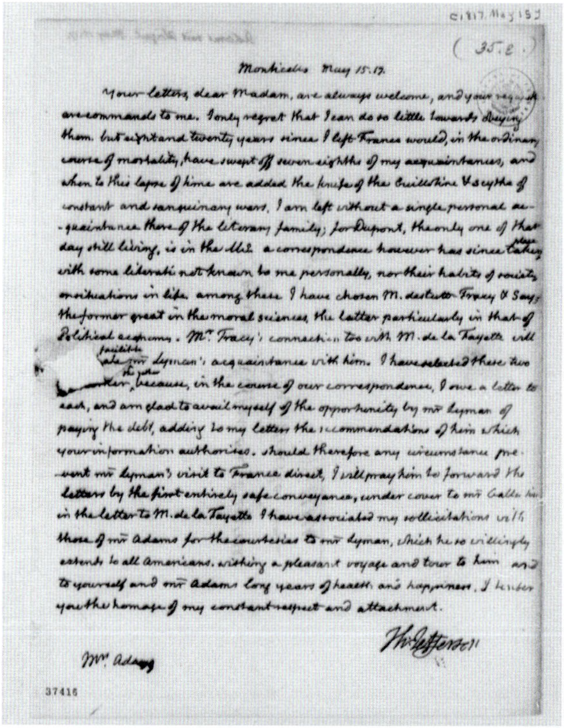

c1817 May 15

(35.e.)

Monticello May 15. 17.

Your letters, dear Madam, are always welcome, and your requests are commands to me. I only regret that I can do so little towards obeying them. but eight and twenty years since I left France would, in the ordinary course of mortality, have swept off seven eighths of my acquaintances, and when to this lapse of time are added the knife of the Guillotine & scythe of constant and sanguinary wars, I am left without a single personal acquaintance there of the literary family; for Dupont, the only one of that day still living, is in the U.S. a correspondence however has since taken place with some literati not known to me personally, nor their habits of society or situations in life. among these I have chosen M. Destutt Tracy & Say; the former great in the moral sciences, the latter particularly in that of Political economy. Mr Tracy's connection too with M. de la Fayette will facilitate mr Lyman's acquaintance with him. I have selected these two the rather, because, in the course of our correspondence, I owe a letter to each, and am glad to avail myself of the opportunity by mr Lyman of paying the debt, adding to my letters the recommendations of him which your information authorises. should therefore any circumstance prevent mr Lyman's visit to France direct, I will pray him to forward the letters by the first entirely safe conveyance, under cover to mr Gallatin. in the letter to M. de la Fayette I have associated my sollicitations with those of mr Adams for the courtesies to mr Lyman, which he so willingly extends to all Americans. wishing a pleasant voyage and tour to him and to yourself and mr Adams long years of health and happiness, I tender you the homage of my constant respect and attachment.

Th: Jefferson

Mrs Adams

37416

1. *Abigail Adams* by Benjamin Blyth. 2. One of the last letters sent by Thomas Jefferson to Abigail Adams, May 1817.
3. Peacefield, the Adams' home in Quincy, Massachusetts.

LESSON 91

1. Read Chapter 16 of *A Child's First.*

   a. Which countries fought in the American Revolutionary War? *The Thirteen United Colonies, England, France, Spain, and Holland. Russia, Denmark, Sweden, Prussia, and Austria formed the League of Armed Neutrality, which also threatened England.*

2. Finish reading *George vs. George.*

   a. Discuss George Washington's refusal to be made king of the United States. What character qualities did this action reveal? How did his choice secure the United States' future as a representative democracy?

   b. Discuss King George's role in the American Revolution. Where do you think he made mistakes? Has this book changed your perceptions of King George in any way? How so? Discuss how information can influence beliefs.

3. Read Chapter 4 and the Afterword of *Remember the Ladies.* This section will take us beyond the current period we are studying, but we will circle back to conclude our study of the American Revolution and the establishment of "a more perfect" nation.

   a. Abigail recognized that access to power could change a person. How did she protect herself from becoming someone different? *She asked her sisters to keep her accountable and tell her if she was changing.*

   b. Etiquette guru Emily Post said that manners and rules of interaction are essential "because they give us confidence, allow our focus to be on the substance of our interactions, and they tell us what to do and what to expect others to do in return." Discuss how the lack of established protocol in the new U.S. government led to awkwardness.

   c. The Adams family made extraordinary sacrifices for the young nation. Discuss the costs of their sacrifice, how the country repaid them, and the Adams family's legacy.

4. Have your student cut out, color, and paste the Abigail Adams picture onto the timeline.

LESSON 92

1. The Americans had won their independence from England, and a new nation had been born! And yet most of the patriots did not think of themselves as citizens of a new country. Their loyalties were with their states. This fractiousness led to many difficulties, culminating in a bloody rebellion led by a soldier named Daniel Shay. Read about how this led to a reexamination of the Articles of Confederation in Chapter 17 of *A Child's First.*

2. To learn more about the Constitution, watch the following: "Constitutional Compromises: Crash Course Government and Politics #5" on the Crash Course YouTube channel and "The Constitutional Convention" on khanacademy.org.

3. Have your student cut out, color, and paste the Victory picture onto the timeline.

LESSON 93

1. Introduce *Shh! We're Writing the Constitution* by Jean Fritz. Read pages 6-13.

    a. What was one of the most significant challenges facing the new nation? *The new country was a collection of sovereign states, each governed separately and with its own regulations, taxation systems, and values. Bringing these independent states together would take a Herculean effort.*

    b. How did Washington's soldiers react to being asked to pledge allegiance to the United States during the Revolutionary War? *They thought Washington was crazy. They were loyal to their home state.*

2. Have your student begin a new section in the notebook and title it "The Federal Government."

3. Watch "Separation of Powers and Checks and Balances: Crash Course Government and Politics #3" on the Crash Course YouTube channel.

LESSON 94

1. Read pages 14-29 of *Shh! We're Writing the Constitution.*

    a. What were the crucial elements of the Virginia Plan presented by Edmund Randolph? *Randolph's plan separated the federal government into three different branches: legislative, executive, and judicial.*

    b. What was James Madison's response to delegates worrying about what "the people" would think of the government the Congress was creating? *Madison understood that the delegates' job was to make the best government possible, not merely please the people.*

    c. What happened to Benjamin Franklin's proposal that Congress begin each day with prayer? *It was debated and tabled.*

    d. What was the Great Compromise? *Every state would be equally represented by two senators in the Senate, while the House of Representatives would reflect each state's population with one representative for every 30,000 inhabitants.*

2. Have your student draw a diagram of the federal government structure using page 15 of *Shh! We're Writing the Constitution* as a guide. Paste the diagram into the notebook.

3. Watch "A More Perfect Union: George Washington and the Making of the Constitution" on George Washington's Mount Vernon YouTube channel.

4. In 1782, the bald eagle was adopted as the national bird. Cut out the bald eagle picture from the Picture Packet, and have your student add it to the notebook along with a few facts from your research.

LESSON 95

1. Read pages 30-35 of *Shh! We're Writing the Constitution.*

   a. How did the delegates deal with the issue of slavery? *They agreed to allow the slave trade until 1808, at which point slavery would continue, but people could no longer buy and sell slaves. We will see that despite this condition, the slave trade continued long after 1808.*

   b. How many states had to ratify the Constitution for it to become the law of the land? *Nine of the thirteen states had to approve. Any state that did not ratify simply would not be part of the new nation.*

   c. What was Madison's argument against a Bill of Rights? *Madison believed that it was clear that individuals kept all the rights that the Constitution didn't specifically give over to the government.*

   d. Benjamin Franklin had a very practical way of looking at the new Constitution. What was it? *It wasn't perfect, but neither was he. No one was perfect, and this document represented the best that they could do.*

   e. What was the final "Big Check" on the power of the federal government to make law? *The Supreme Court.*

2. Have your student cut out, color, and paste the Second Continental Congress picture onto the timeline.

LESSON 96

1. Finish reading *Shh! We're Writing the Constitution.* The entirety of the U.S. Constitution appears at the back of this book. Review the Bill of Rights with your student. Which rights do you think were most important to list?

2. Watch "A 3-minute guide to the Bill of Rights–Belinda Stutzman" on the TedEd YouTube channel.

3. Have your student cut out, color, and paste the Bill of Rights picture onto the timeline.

As you have seen in *Shh! We're Writing the Constitution,* the process of creating a government was one fraught with disagreement, debate, and compromise. Thomas Jefferson was correct when he stated that the Constitution was "unquestionably the wisest ever yet presented to men." Benjamin Franklin was also right when he said it was not perfect. Both men, and all the delegates involved, knew that changes would have to be made to the Constitution as the nation grew and changed. The amendment process guards against frivolous changes while providing an avenue for the Constitution to be improved. The Constitution is a remarkable document in human history, and thanks to the people who continue to work for justice and freedom, it continues to be the basis by which we citizens strive toward a more perfect Union.

Historic Table

Chicken Madeira

The founding fathers' fondness for Portuguese Madeira wine made this a wildly popular dish in its day. It is relatively simple and generally enjoyed by all ages. Portuguese Madeira—imported from the island off the coast of Africa—became all the rage in the late 1700s. On the transatlantic voyage, the casks stored on deck were subject to rain, sun, and saltwater spray, which seemed to improve the wine's quality and sweetness. It became known as "Rainwater Madeira" and is the wine the founders toasted with when they approved the Declaration of Independence in 1776. If Madeira is unavailable, a Marsala or port wine will do. For the beef demi-glace, a premade brown gravy will work, or Savory Choice has a beef demi-glace available at many grocery stores. Use any variety of mushrooms. This recipe is adapted from *A Taste of History* on PBS.

4 chicken breasts, sliced lengthwise
sprigs of fresh basil, rosemary, thyme, marjoram
2 cups of mushrooms, sliced—any combination of cremini,
oyster, baby bella, porcini, royal trumpet, or maitake
4-6 tablespoons butter
white flour for dipping
salt and pepper
box of beef demi-glace or brown gravy to equal 1 cup
1 cup Rainwater Madeira
fresh parsley for garnish

Directions:

Place breasts in a bowl. Finely chop a mixture of basil, rosemary, thyme, and marjoram, and add to bowl. Then sprinkle the breasts with Rainwater Madeira, toss, and marinate for at least a few hours or overnight. Pat breasts partially dry, sprinkle with salt and pepper, and dip lightly in flour. Heat butter and brown breasts quickly in butter. Do not cook, just brown. Set chicken aside. Add mushrooms to the remaining butter, adding more if necessary. Sauté mushrooms at high heat until brown. Return chicken to the pan and add 1 cup Madeira. Simmer and then add beef demi-glace or brown gravy to equal 3/4 cups. Simmer for about 10 minutes or until thickened and then serve with mashed potatoes. If you want to make the potato cakes shown here, check out this recipe: www.allrecipes.com/recipe/223597/old-fashioned-potato-cakes/

The Oregon Trail by Albert Bierstadt, 1869

The Young United States

After five long years of war, Americans entered the post-war era with a profound sense of possibility, innovation, and hope. The United States was like an enthusiastic young adult ready to embrace newfound freedom and opportunity. Industry and innovation flourished. Enhancing this hopeful backdrop, Thomas Jefferson negotiated the Louisiana Purchase, doubling the size of our republic, and making land ownership a possibility for countless Americans. We will explore how the Lewis and Clark Expedition of 1804 was a pivotal moment in opening up this rich territory for eager settlers and pioneers.

Post-war industries, including whaling, flourished in the north as technological innovation created industrial cities and established the United States as an economic force. The discovery of gold in California ushered in a massive movement of settlers to the West and created a need for links between the Pacific and Atlantic. The Pony Express filled that gap for a brief but nearly mythological eighteen months before being replaced by the telegraph. Soon the nation's shores were linked by the Transcontinental Railroad, firmly establishing the continental nature of the United States.

The thirst for land meant that hundreds of thousands of Indigenous people were driven off their ancestral lands and relocated to reservations, where their traditions and cultural practices were threatened and often lost. We will look at the Trail of Tears and how the western movement forever altered the lives of the diverse tribes who had called this country home long before European arrival.

In the South, the freedom that Americans fought so sacrificially for was not extended to the enslaved populations working the fields, homes, and plantation industries driving the post-war boom. For freedom-loving groups like the Quakers and abolitionists, the plight of these men, women, and children—nearly twenty percent of the country's population—drove their passion to see slavery abolished. This led to the expansion and development of the Underground Railroad, and voices like Frederick Douglass, Sojourner Truth, and William Lloyd Garrison were heard around the country. We will learn their stories and study the life of one of America's most courageous and effective warriors in the fight for abolition—Harriet Tubman.

Rabbit Trails

Red Cloud and *Buffalo Bird Girl* by S. D. Nelson
Tell the tales of two iconic Indigenous People—a Lakota chief and a young Hidatsa girl. See also Nelson's *Sitting Bull* and *Black Elk's Vision.*

Dave the Potter: Artist, Poet, Slave by Laban Carrick
The inspiring true story of one of America's greatest potters—a slave who not only crafted works of art but inscribed them with verses about nature, divinity, and faith.

The Journey of York: The Unsung Hero of the Lewis & Clark Expedition by Hasan Davis
Relates how York did not choose to join the expedition; he could not because he was a slave. But his contributions to the expedition are now becoming known, and he is finally getting his due.

Mumbet's Declaration of Independence by Gretchen Woelfle
The true story of a slave who had the courage and audacity to use the newly drafted Massachusetts Constitution to sue for and win her freedom.

Mark Twain and the Queens of the Mississippi by Cheryl Harness
Tells the story of one of America's great rivers through the eyes and words of one of America's greatest writers—Samuel Clemens.

Noah Webster and His Words by Jeri Chase Ferris
Tells how Webster saw that nothing could unite the newly formed country more effectively than a dictionary that would standardize American language and spelling! He was right!

The Young United States by Edwin Tunis
Explores the changing, growing, thriving new democracy through 450 exquisite drawings and intriguing text.

Crafts & Projects

Build a Corps of Discovery Diorama

If you would like to build a Lewis and Clark Expedition diorama, Imex makes one titled Lewis & Clark Expedition Set IMXS0523. It is available on Amazon or at Hobby Lobby. These are tiny miniatures that are historically accurate and include the key Corps members, Sacagawea, canoes, tepees, horses, and so forth. If you have a student that loves to work with tiny miniature worlds, this would be an enjoyable project to do together.

A Sailor's Life for Me

Play this online game to learn about life aboard a nineteenth-century ship: https://asailorslifeforme.org/

Build a Model Whaler

There are several inexpensive kits on Amazon and other online retailers. Look for the "Academy New Bedford Whaler Model Kit" or the "Cutty Sark Clipper Ship Model Kit."

Make a 3D Globe

This website explores the difficulty cartographers face in creating globes and how distorted our perceptions of the continents' shapes and sizes are due to this challenge: www.3dgeography.co.uk/make-a-globe

Gold Rush

Channel your inner '49er and try your hand at panning for gold. This great how-to guide will get you started: https://runwildmychild.com/panning-for-gold

Recommended Readers

Fever: 1793 by Laurie Halse Anderson

Soft Rain: A Story of the Cherokee Trail of Tears by Cornelia Cornelissen

Kit Carson and the Wild Frontier by Ralph Moody

Caddie Woodlawn by Carol Ryrie Brink

The Birchbark House by Louise Erdrich

Dr. Jenner and the Speckled Monster by Albert Marrin

The Tragic Tale of Narcissa Whitman by Cheryl Harness

Amistad: A Long Road to Freedom by Walter Dean Myers

The Cabin Faced West by Jean Fritz

Online Resources

Follow the Corps of Discovery. Visit the Monticello website to access an interactive map to discover some of the artifacts the Corps sent to President Jefferson:
www.monticello.org/research-education/for-educators/interactive-posters/lewis-and-clark-artifacts-at-monticello/

Take a virtual tour of *Old Ironsides*: https://ussconstitutionmuseum.org/

Explore the Alamo. The Alamo's website provides detailed lesson plans on the history of this storied landmark for those who want to dig deeper: www.thealamo.org/remember/education/lesson-plans/index.html

Whaling Perspectives: The Providence Public Library Special Collections blog has a collection of beautiful, detailed, and fascinating illustrations, paintings, and scrimshaw art that is well worth perusing:
https://pplspcoll.wordpress.com/2014/11/13/saltwatercolors/

Underground Railroad: Learning to Give has several in-depth units on the Underground Railroad, people involved in it, Harriet Tubman, and more! Simply search "Underground Railroad" at learningtogive.org.

The National Parks Service: Check out stops on the Underground Railroad near you! The NPS has an extensive library of resources for learning more about the Underground Railroad. Look at its"Lesson Plans" under "Kids and Education" to see if there is a park near you: www.nps.gov/subjects/undergroundrailroad/index.htm

Character Connection: Love

God is love, and as his followers, we are to show his love to those around us. This section includes some amazing stories of people who were motivated by love to pursue justice and righteousness for their neighbors. Use the following Bible verses to discuss the cost of love and its power to transform as you study the stories in this section:

Psalm 116:1-2
Proverbs 3:3-4
Proverbs 10:12
Lamentations 3:22-23
Matthew 5:44
Mark 12:13
John 15:13
Romans 12:9-10
1 Corinthians 13:1-5
1 Corinthians 18:14
1 Timothy 4:12
2 Timothy 1:7
1 John 4:16-20
1 John 4:8-9
1 Peter 4:8

LESSON 97

1. Read Chapters 18 and 19 of *A Child's First.*

a. Today it is common for First Ladies to use their clothing choices to make political statements or promote American designers. What message did George Washington's inaugural suit send? *George Washington's plain suit was made entirely in the young United States, showing he supported American industry. The following point is not made in the text, but it is historical: Washington chose to wear his humble suit to convey that he was one of the people and not a king in regalia.* To learn more, read the following account of George Washington's inauguration:
www.thedailybeast.com/george-washington-and-the-story-of-the-first-inaugural-address

2. Have your student begin a new section in the notebook titled "The Lewis and Clark Expedition." Cut out the Louisiana Purchase map in the Picture Packet, and paste it in the notebook.

LESSON 98

1. Introduce *How We Crossed the West* by Rosalyn Schanzer, and study the map on pages 2-3. Locate the 13 different Indigenous tribes depicted on the map. Study the expedition's path (marked in red) from where it starts at Camp Wood to where it ends at Fort Clatsop.

a. What natural landform does each part of the journey follow? Why do you think this is so? *The explorers followed the paths of rivers for the entire expedition. Rivers are natural highways because they are often navigable by boat, which makes travel faster.*

2. Read "A Note from the Author" and the next five pages.

a. What was the author's goal in telling this story? *Ms. Schanzer wanted to tell the story as authentically as possible by using the Corps of Discovery members' original words.*

b. Why did President Thomas Jefferson commission the Corps of Discovery? *He hoped to find a water route leading westward, develop friendly relations with Native tribes, create maps, and explore and record the flora and fauna.*

c. Study the descriptions of the men who made up the Corps. What type of men were they? *Lewis and Clark were looking for hearty men with wilderness skills, familiarity with Native ways, experienced hunters, woodsmen, rivermen, and even blacksmiths and gunsmiths. One even knew "hand talk" or sign language.*

LESSON 99

1. Read from "May 14, 1804," through "October 9, 1804," in *How We Crossed the West.*

a. Describe the hardships of the first days of the expedition. *Mosquitos and ticks plagued the men, and the boat's mast broke on a sycamore limb.*

b. Describe the abundance of wildlife the men encountered. *The men easily caught plump catfish, turkey, geese, and beaver. There were also vast herds of buffalo and antelope.*

c. Why were Lewis and Clark unable to find the Omaha? *Many Omaha had died due to smallpox.*

d. What happened in the section titled "Trouble" that made Partizan threaten the expedition? *Partizan did not feel they had given him enough gifts.*

2. Cut out the bison and prairie dog images from the Picture Packet, and have your student color and add them to the notebook along with a few facts from your research.

LESSON 100

1. Read from "Building Fort Mandan" through "Two Narrow Escapes" of *How We Crossed the West.*

    a. How did Lewis and Clark describe the Mandan? *They found them to be the friendliest Indians they had met on the Missouri River.*

    b. Why did Mr. Toussaint Charbonneau come to Fort Mandan? How could his wife, Sacagawea, be particularly helpful? *Charbonneau was looking for a job as an interpreter. Sacagawea was a Shoshoni from the Rocky Mountains and would be able to procure horses to cross the mountains.*

    c. What was extraordinary about the winter of 1804-1805? What did Lewis and Clark observe about Indians' tolerance of cold temperatures? *The winter of 1804-1805 was frigid, with temperatures in the –40° range. Not only did the Indians seem able to tolerate the cold better than the white men, but they could stay exposed to extreme cold without frostbite.*

    d. When the squall hits the pirogue, how does Sacagawea's calm fortitude save the day? *Though Charbonneau panicked and nearly overturned the pirogue, Sacagawea remained calm and rescued most of the equipment that was floating in the water.*

2. Have your student cut out, color, and paste the Corps of Discovery picture onto the timeline.

3. Cut out the beaver and the grizzly bear images from the Picture Packet, and have your student color and add them to the notebook along with a few facts from your research.

LESSON 101

1. Read "The Great Falls of the Missouri" to the conclusion of *How We Crossed the West.*

    a. What did Captain Lewis consider the "grandest sight [he] ever beheld?" *Lewis was amazed by the enormous cascading wall of water at the Great Falls of Missouri.*

    b. What serendipitous meeting gave Sacagawea great joy? How did the Shoshoni help the expedition? *Sacagawea reunited with the Shoshoni and her brother, Chief Cameahwait, whom she had not seen since being kidnapped as a young girl. The Shoshoni helped the expedition by providing horses and warning them of the route's difficulty and the lack of game to hunt.*

    c. When the expedition crossed the Bitterroot Mountains, was the counsel of the Shoshoni proven accurate? *Yes, the crossing was extremely arduous. They lost several horses due to the treacherous conditions and had to eat others for lack of game to hunt.*

    d. How did the Nez Perce help the expedition? *They escorted the men to the Grand Chief's lodge, where he drew a map to guide the expedition.*

    e. What was a unique practice of the Chinook Indians? *The Chinook flattened the heads of the children so that their foreheads sloped back at an unusual angle. (Historians believe this custom demonstrates the person was free, not a captive.) Note the picture and the unique cradleboard used to achieve sloping the forehead.*

1. *Chinook Mother and Child* by Paul Kane, 1848. 2. Mandan Chief Sheheke who traveled with Lewis and Clark.
3. *The Scouts* by Charles M. Russell.

LESSON 101 continued

2. Cut out the snow goose and the mountain goat images from the Picture Packet, and have your student color and add them to the notebook along with a few facts from your research.

3. To conclude your study of the Lewis and Clark Expedition, consider watching the following excellent productions: *Lewis and Clark: The Journey of the Corps of Discovery* by Ken Burns, available for a rental fee on Amazon or free with a subscription to PBS. *Or Perish in the Attempt: The Story of the Medicine of Lewis and Clark* is also available on PBS.

4. After viewing one of the productions above, have your student study the final two pages of *How We Crossed the West* and write a report highlighting the Corps of Discovery's key accomplishments.

LESSON 102

1. The Corps of Discovery opened northern territories to further exploration and settlement by Americans, but there was trouble brewing with Britain. This would lead to the War of 1812, one of the most error-riddled conflicts in American history during which the British burned Washington, D.C. To learn more about it, access one of the following videos.

    "When the British burned the White House" on the CBS Sunday Morning YouTube channel

    "War of 1812 in 12 Minutes - Manny Man Does History" on the John D Ruddy YouTube channel

    "The War of 1812 - Crash Course US History #11" on the Crash Course YouTube channel provides an irreverent, rollicking overview.

2. Read Chapter 20 of *A Child's First.*

3. Have your student cut out, color, and paste the War of 1812 picture onto the timeline.

4. If desired, have your student write out the words to "The Star Spangled Banner" by Francis Scott Key in the notebook.

LESSON 103

1. Read Chapter 21 of *A Child's First* to learn more about the fur trappers and trailblazers who expanded the areas explored by Lewis and Clark.

2. The expansion of U.S. territory pushed forward a moral issue that the nation had avoided for too long: slavery. Abolitionists were gaining strength in their fight against this evil, and one of the strong voices leading the charge against slavery belonged to Sojourner Truth. Learn more about her remarkable life by watching "The electrifying speeches of Sojourner Truth–Daina Ramey Berry" on the TedEd YouTube channel.

3. To learn more about Sojourner's life story, access the following free graphic novel, which captures the drama of her story using many of her own words: https://en.unesco.org/womeninafrica/sites/default/files/pdf/Sojourner%20Truth_Women%20in%20African%20History_Comic%20Strip.pdf

4. Have your student cut out, color, and paste the Abolitionist Movement picture onto the timeline. You will learn more about Frederick Douglass and William Lloyd Garrison later in the study.

LESSON 104

1. In the graphic novel on Sojourner Truth, we learned that she understood photography to be a powerful medium for communication. Over 150 years later, Sojourner Truth is still inspiring art. Watch the following video to see how her life story inspires the artist Grace Lynne Haynes: www.newyorker.com/video/watch/why-a-prominent-american-artist-paints-skin-pitch-black

2. Have your student create a collage painting of a historical figure from this study using the techniques described by Grace Lynne Haynes in the video.

3. Read Chapter 22 of *A Child's First.* Discuss why the settling of the nation required both "brawn and brains."

LESSON 105

1. Read Chapters 23 and 24 of *A Child's First.*

2. As the United States pushed its borders west, it forced Indigenous Peoples and nations off their lands. George Washington had foreseen this and tried to prevent it from happening during his first term in office, but there had been no political support for his ideas. So, despite the efforts of our nation's father, approximately 100,000 Cherokee, Muscogee, Seminole, Chickasaw, and Choctaw were forcibly removed from their ancestral lands and made to march hundreds of miles to reservations west of the Mississippi River. To learn more, watch the following: www.cherokeehistorical.org/unto-these-hills/trail-of-tears/

3. Have your student cut out, color, and paste the Trail of Tears picture onto the timeline.

LESSON 106

1. Read Chapter 26 of *A Child's First.* Skip Chapter 25 for now, as we will be returning to it later.

2. Our next title is *Heart of a Samurai* by Margi Preus. This book follows the true story of a Japanese boy shipwrecked off the coast of Japan and rescued by the captain of an American whaling ship. This fascinating story provides an outsider's perspective on the young United States. The text is divided into four lessons so the reading sections will be longer than usual. To facilitate the reading, there are discussion prompts but not comprehension questions. Take your time with the next few lessons, spreading them over a few weeks. Read Parts One and Two.

Discussion prompts:

a. Manjiro lived in Japan at a time when it had been closed to outsiders for two centuries. How did this shape his view of foreigners?

b. Manjiro's curiosity was unique among his companions. How did it set him apart? Discuss his companions' discouragement of his inquisitive personality and what it reveals about their culture. How can respect for authority discourage questioning?

c. Discuss Captain Whitfield's character. Which character traits stand out the most and how are they reflected in *A Psalm for Life* by Henry Wadsworth Longfellow? You can read the entire poem here: www.poetryfoundation.org/poems/44644/a-psalm-of-life. Have your student copy the poem into the notebook and memorize, if desired.

1. Captain Whitfield. 2. *Lancing a Sperm Whale* by Clifford Ashley.

LESSON 106 continued

Resources for further exploration:

Japan:
Watch the following short lecture explaining why Japan closed its borders to the world: "Japanese Isolation" on the Joshua Downey YouTube channel.

Whaling:
One of the largest industries in the nineteenth century was whaling. It was uniquely egalitarian, as any strong man could join a whaling ship and have an opportunity to make a living. This meant that it attracted Black freedmen and runaways who were looking for a new livelihood. To read more about this, check out *Black Hands, White Sails: The Story of African American Whalers* by Patricia C. McKissack and Fredrick L. McKissack.

Girl on a Whaleship features the journals of a six-year-old girl who joined her family on a whaleship in the Pacific Ocean. You can read her diaries, access detailed information on whaling and its history, and much more here: www.girlonawhaleship.org

Access teaching resources from the New Bedford Whaling Museum here:
https://educators.whalingmuseum.org/resources.html

Explore the *Charles W. Morgan*, a whaling ship much like the *John Howland*:
https://educators.mysticseaport.org/artifacts/cwm_ship/

3. Cut out the right whale image from the Picture Packet and have your student color and add it to the notebook along with a few facts from your research.

LESSON 107

1. Read Part Three of *Heart of a Samurai.*

a. Describe Manjiro's American experience. How was the United States different from Japan?

b. Why does Manjiro feel that he has been "transformed from a poor fisherman into a prince"?

c. Discuss Manjiro's experience at church in Fairhaven. How did the people in the first two churches he attended treat him? How did this violate James 1:2-4?

d. Manjiro discovered that beauty and pain often accompany one another. How did he gain this wisdom?

Resources for further exploration:

Life in a Seaport: Experience what life would have been like in a seaport in the nineteenth century to understand more of Manjiro's experience by making a virtual visit to Mystic Seaport, Connecticut: www.mysticseaport.org/explore/village/

Manjiro in Fairhaven: https://fairhaventours.com/manjiro-nakahama/

2. Read Chapter 27 of *A Child's First* to learn about the ill-fated Donner party that began their journey west the same year that Manjiro signed on to sail aboard the *Franklin.*

LESSON 108

1. Read Part Four of *Heart of a Samurai.* Discussion prompts:

 a. What dream never left Manjiro? How did this dream guide his decision to sign on to another whaling expedition?

 b. What painful realization did Manjiro come to on pages 218-219? Discuss how you would feel in Manjiro's place.

Resources for further exploration:

 The Whitfield-Manjiro Friendship Society preserves the memory of this vital friendship and maintains landmarks central to Manjiro and Captain Whitfield's stories. Learn more here: https://whitfield-manjiro.org/

 Hawaii: Manjiro's Japanese companions spent several years living in the nation of Hawaii before it was annexed to the United States. Read more about Hawaii's fascinating history at the following resources: www.gohawaii.com/hawaiian-culture/history https://ushistoryscene.com/article/aloha-hawaii/

 Manjiro: Drifting, 1841–2020: Take a virtual visit to this gallery exhibition of Manjiro's artwork and writing. Click on the PDF to access the exhibit and scroll down several pages to see Manjiro's artwork. **Note:** There is an image with historically accurate nudity. https://rosenbach.org/visit/exhibitions/manjiro-drifting-1841-2020/

2. The sperm whale was highly prized by whalers for both its oil and spermaceti. Cut out the sperm whale image from the Picture Packet, and have your student color and add it to the notebook along with a few facts from your research.

3. Read Chapter 28 of *A Child's First* to learn about the California Gold Rush. Manjiro saw the California Gold Rush as an unparalleled opportunity to earn the money he needed to return to his homeland. Thousands of other people also saw a path to fortune and prosperity in the Sierra Nevada Mountains.

4. Have your student cut out, color, and paste the Gold Rush picture onto the timeline.

LESSON 109

1. Read Part Five, Epilogue, and the Historical Note of *Heart of a Samurai.* Discussion prompts:

 a. Discuss Manjiro's desire to bring change to Japan. Do you think he succeeded? How?

 b. Discuss how Manjiro changed over the course of this story. How did his seashell collection symbolize his growing understanding of humanity?

2. Have your student choose a topic from the following list to research and prepare a presentation. The presentation should include background information, historical context, maps, artwork (if relevant), and explanatory narration. Your student should conduct research over the next week and make their presentation the following week.

 The life and adventures of Manjiro
 Nineteenth-century whaling
 The California Gold Rush

3. Watch a video representation of Manjiro's autobiography: "Japanese Castaway Gives First Description of USA (1852) // Incredible Story of John Manjiro" on the Voices of the Past YouTube channel.

LESSON 110

1. Read Chapter 29 of *A Child's First* to learn about the Mexican-American War, decried by Abraham Lincoln as "unnecessarily and unconstitutionally commenced."

2. It is time to go back and read Chapter 25 in *A Child's First.* We will be exploring slavery and the Underground Railroad in the next several lessons.

3. Choose an activity from the Crafts and Projects or Online Resources (pages 105-106) to enjoy with your student.

LESSON 111

1. Introduce *Harriet Tubman: Conductor on the Underground Railroad* by Kate McMullan. Read pages 1-15.

   a. Harriet "Minty" Tubman was born into slavery. One of the hardships of slavery was the practice of masters hiring out their slaves to make money. When Minty was hired out to the Cook family, she became so sick she nearly died. Describe the conditions that led to Minty becoming so ill. *Though Minty was just a child, she was forced to wade into cold water all day, barefoot and without proper clothing. Even when she had a fever, Mr. Cook forced Minty to work. This exposure led to her contracting measles and bronchitis.*

   b. What do you think was especially cruel about Minty's treatment at Miss Susan's home? How did Miss Emily show some empathy to Minty? *Miss Susan cruelly punished Minty for not cleaning correctly, even though she had failed to teach her how. Miss Emily showed empathy by training Minty how to clean properly.*

   c. How was Miss Susan unreasonable when she demanded Minty keep the baby quiet through the night? *Most babies wake up due to hunger. Making Minty responsible for keeping the infant quiet when she had no way to feed her was inhumane to both the infant and Minty.*

   d. It has often been said that slavery dehumanizes the slave and the master alike. Based on the reading so far, discuss the evil of slavery in light of the maxim, "Power corrupts. Absolute power corrupts absolutely."

LESSON 112

1. Read pages 16-32 of *Harriet Tubman: Conductor on the Underground Railroad.*

   a. What happened in the 1830s that gave hope to enslaved people? Discuss the power of hope. *Abolitionists worked together to create the Underground Railroad to help slaves escape. The hope of deliverance can help make terrible circumstances endurable.*

   b. In 1831, Nat Turner had a vision that he believed was from God. Discuss the controversial aspects of this. *Nat Turner believed God called him to end slavery and had instructed him to kill all the white people he could. Think about Nat's claim to be a prophet and the commandment, "Thou shalt not kill." Others have argued that slavery is so egregious that the taking of human life is justified, as it would be in war.*

   c. How were slaves further restricted following the Nat Turner rebellion? *Slaves were forbidden to meet for worship; even meeting together to talk was not allowed, and teaching slaves to read and write became illegal.*

LESSON 112 continued

d. Minty suffered an injury to her brain that caused her to remain in a coma for some time. Today, we know that she suffered a traumatic brain injury that would occasionally cause sudden lapses in consciousness even after recovering. Consider this disability in light of the fact that Harriet was never apprehended while helping slaves to escape.

e. Describe some of the things Harriet's father taught her about nature. *He helped her identify the North Star, imitate bird calls, and know which berries were safe or poisonous. He taught her how to move through the forest silently and to identify north when it was cloudy.*

f. Though Harriet married John Tubman, she was still at risk of being sold south. Why? *Marriage licenses of slaves were not honored by most slave masters, and even though her husband was free, Harriet still belonged to Mr. Stewart, who could sell her south at any time.*

2. Have your student cut out, color, and paste the Underground Railroad picture onto the timeline.

3. Choose an activity from the Crafts and Projects or Online Resources (pages 105-106).

LESSON 113

1. Read pages 33-55 of *Harriet Tubman: Conductor on the Underground Railroad.*

a. Over the years, Harriet had many frightening dreams. In the chapter "Go Free or Die," the thing she feared most came upon her. What was it? Once her fate was sure, what did Harriet decide to do? *Harriet had many dreams of being sold south, and this dream (or nightmare) became a reality. Once she learned she and her brothers would be sold south, she convinced her brothers to join her, but they became too frightened and refused to go on. She had to press on alone.*

b. Consider how many different people and how many coordinated efforts it took to help Harriet reach freedom in Philadelphia. Describe the emotional highs and lows Harriet felt when she realized freedom was hers. What did she promise herself? *Harriet felt such a glory over everything; she felt as though she were in heaven. Shortly after, her heart fell because it dawned on her that there was no one to welcome her—she was a stranger in a strange land. She vowed she would return and bring her family out of bondage.*

2. The Secretary of the Pennsylvania Anti-Slavery Society, William Still, helped Harriet when she first arrived in Philadelphia and throughout her many missions to the South. Still's meticulous record-keeping (at much risk to himself) has been invaluable in piecing together Underground Railroad history. PBS has an hour-long film on the life of Still, the Fugitive Slave Act, and the Underground Railroad. Look for *Underground Railroad: The William Still Story* on pbs.org.

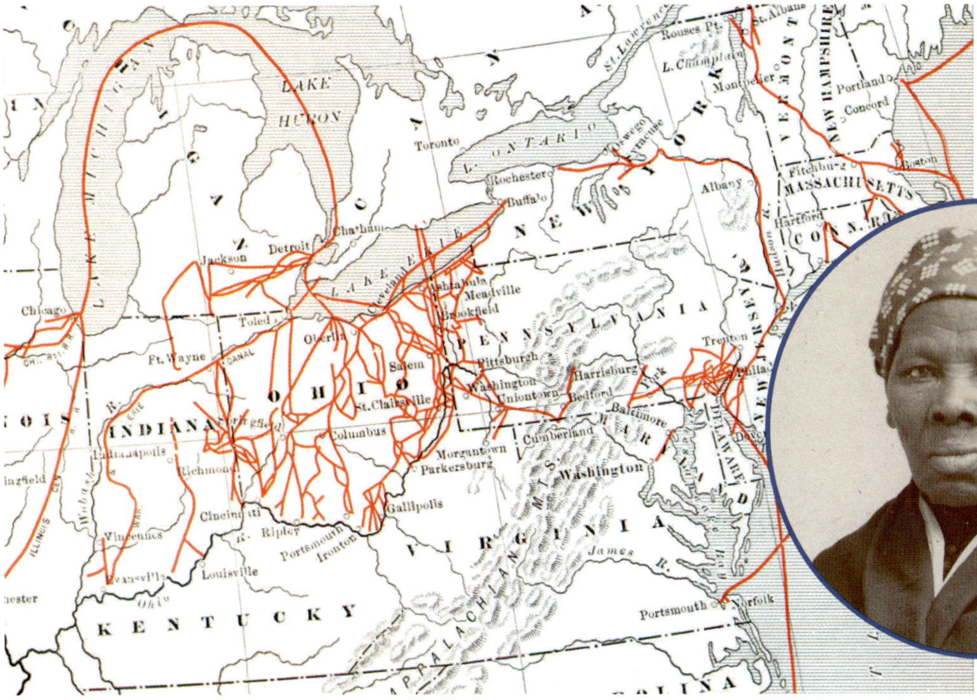

1. *The Fugitive Slaves* by Eastman Johnson. 2. Map showing routes on the Underground Railroad. 3. Harriet Tubman.

LESSON 114

1. Read pages 56-71 of *Harriet Tubman: Conductor on the Underground Railroad.*

   a. Describe why the Fugitive Slave Act was so devastating to freed slaves. How did the Act affect the Underground Railroad? Why did corrupt commissioners declare most Blacks were runaway slaves? *The Fugitive Slave Act made it the duty of all citizens, even those living in free northern states, to help capture runaways. Suddenly, even those like Harriet, who had escaped to a free state, were now in danger. Those who refused to obey this new law would be subject to fines and imprisonment. This Act severely hampered the Underground Railroad because harboring or aiding runaway slaves could result in severe penalties and prison. Corrupt commissioners earned twice the amount to declare that Blacks were runaways, which resulted in many free Blacks being sent south.*

   b. Why do you think many people began to believe that Moses was a man? *As legends began to circulate about "Moses," people assumed only a powerful man could steal away "property" as quickly and expertly as Harriet did.*

2. Visit mission-us.org for an interactive game that simulates helping a 14-year-old enslaved girl named Lucy King find a path to freedom. The game, *1848: The Antebellum Era: Flight to Freedom*, takes about two hours as the player makes choices for Lucy to help her achieve her goal in the face of historical realities.

LESSON 115

1. Read pages 72-94 of *Harriet Tubman: Conductor on the Underground Railroad.*

   a. How does the Charles Nalle case demonstrate the evil of the Fugitive Slave Act? *Though Nalle had escaped enslavement, he could be apprehended and returned to slavery at any time. Even when abolitionists raised the money to purchase him, the judge still ordered him returned to his master.*

   b. The Charles Nalle courtroom scene demonstrated the devotion of the abolitionists. How? *Abolitionists were willing to lay down their own lives for the freedom of another, and many did so in order to free Mr. Nalle.*

   c. Why was Harriet's work with former slaves so essential during the Civil War? *Because Northern and Southern dialects were so different, Harriet was able to act as an intermediary between recently freed slaves and the Union Army. Harriet also nursed the sick and wounded at field hospitals and used Rit's herbal remedies to help those suffering from dysentery. She also began small wartime businesses to help employ former slaves who desperately needed work.*

   d. Describe why Harriet's work as Commander of Intelligence Operations for the Union Army's Department of the South was an extraordinary moment in history. *Harriet commanded river pilots and nine scouts. None of these men had ever served under a woman, let alone a Black woman.*

   e. Why was the capture of the Combahee Confederate encampment by Harriet and her men so remarkable? *Harriet and her Union soldiers surprised the camp and captured it without firing a single shot.*

   f. What was the tragic irony in Harriet's train trip home at the end of the war? *Though Harriet had served the Union cause with courage, selflessness, and honor, the train conductor treated her shamefully and inhumanely on her trip home, revealing that though slavery was dead, racism was very much alive.*

LESSON 116

1. Conclude the reading of *Harriet Tubman: Conductor on the Underground Railroad.*

    a. Describe why the government's refusal to pay Harriet the money they owed for her Union Army service was shameful. What do you think it reveals about the government's highest offices at that time?

2. Conclude your study of Harriet Tubman by having the student cut out, color, and paste Harriet's picture from the Picture Packet in the notebook. Record Harriet's statement about her work as a conductor on the Underground Railroad (from page 99) in the notebook. Then, have your student write a brief biography of Harriet's life and record a final draft in the notebook. Then, have your student cut out, color, and paste the Harriet Tubman picture onto the timeline.

LESSON 117

1. The Fugitive Slave Act was passed in 1850. We learned about how the incredible injustice of this law motivated abolitionists in their battle against slavery. One of those abolitionists was a woman who was already active in the Underground Railroad, Harriet Beecher Stowe. She wrote a book called *Uncle Tom's Cabin* that captured the plight of enslaved people and opened thousands of people's eyes to the injustices of slavery. Learn more by watching the following videos at khanacademy.org:
    "Uncle Tom's Cabin - influence of the Fugitive Slave Act"
    "Uncle Tom's Cabin - reception and significance"

2. Have your student cut out, color, and paste the picture of Harriet Beecher Stowe on the timeline.

The Repatriation of the Captives by Hale Woodruff, 1943

In 1838, a 25-year-old enslaved Mendeian named Cinque led a successful revolt aboard the Spanish slave ship *La Amistad*. After killing the ship's crew, the rebels ordered their surviving captors to turn back to Africa, though the schooner eventually anchored near Long Island. The U.S. government towed the ship to New London, Connecticut, and charged its "cargo" with piracy and murder. Luckily, abolitionists caught wind of the case, and after a few years, the prisoners were freed and sent back home.

Historic Table

Chicken Fricassee

This dish was widely popular in the first decades of our nation's history, and its many adaptations reflect the cultural influences shaping the nation in the nineteenth century. Presidents from Washington to Lincoln all counted it as a favorite. Lafayette was so delighted by this dish that he asked Martha Washington to send the recipe to his wife. Originating in France and adapted by a diverse range of Spanish, Creole, Jewish, English, and African cooks, this dish is a great example of the melting pot nature of American cuisine. This recipe is adapted from delish.com.

2 tablespoons olive oil
2 pounds skin-on, bone-in chicken thighs
Kosher salt
Freshly ground black pepper
2 tablespoons butter
1 large onion, chopped
1 large carrot, peeled and chopped
1 celery stalk, chopped
8 ounces mushrooms, sliced
2 tablespoons all-purpose flour
1/2 cup white wine (optional)
2 cups chicken broth
1 cup heavy cream
2 tablespoons freshly chopped parsley
2 teaspoons freshly chopped thyme leaves

Heat the oil in a large, high-sided skillet over medium heat. Season chicken on both sides with salt and pepper, and then add to skillet and cook until golden, 5 minutes per side. Remove from skillet and set aside. In the same skillet, melt butter and add onion, carrot, celery, and mushrooms, and cook until soft, 5 minutes. Whisk in flour till smooth, and cook for 1 minute. Pour in the wine and scrape up any bits on the bottom of the pan, and reduce wine by half, about 7 minutes. Add broth and cream, and season with parsley, thyme, and salt and pepper to taste. Add chicken back to pan and simmer until chicken is cooked through and sauce is thickened, about 20-30 minutes.

The Civil War

The expansion of the United States through the Louisiana Purchase and the westward movement of pioneers and settlers brought the issue of slavery to the political forefront. The decision about whether new states joining the Union would be slave or free pushed the nation relentlessly and irrevocably toward a rupture. The work of abolitionists was effectively changing hearts and minds in the North while the expanding territories forced the South to fight for states' rights to protect the institution of slavery.

Upon this scene, Abraham Lincoln was elected the sixteenth president. He had made his views clear that "a house divided against itself cannot stand." Regardless, Southern states began to secede from the Union, so that within three months, seven had done so, and just over a month after Lincoln's inauguration, war was declared. Fortunately for this nation, Lincoln had the wisdom and foresight to see the Union preserved and slavery abolished—but not before four long years of bloodshed and devastation. The Civil War was not only the deadliest war in American history but also the most tragic because the citizens of our nation were pitted against one another.

As in any war, there are shining stories of courage and selfless devotion that emerge and become part of the fabric of who we are as a people: Lincoln's grit in the face of continual assassination threats; the heroism of Massachusetts's 54th Black regiment; the audacity of Robert Smalls, the enslaved boat pilot who commandeered a Confederate ship into Union hands; and the spunk of Johnny Lincoln Clem who joined the Union cause at age nine. By learning their stories, we honor their sacrifice. And we learn to value the freedom they paid so dearly for.

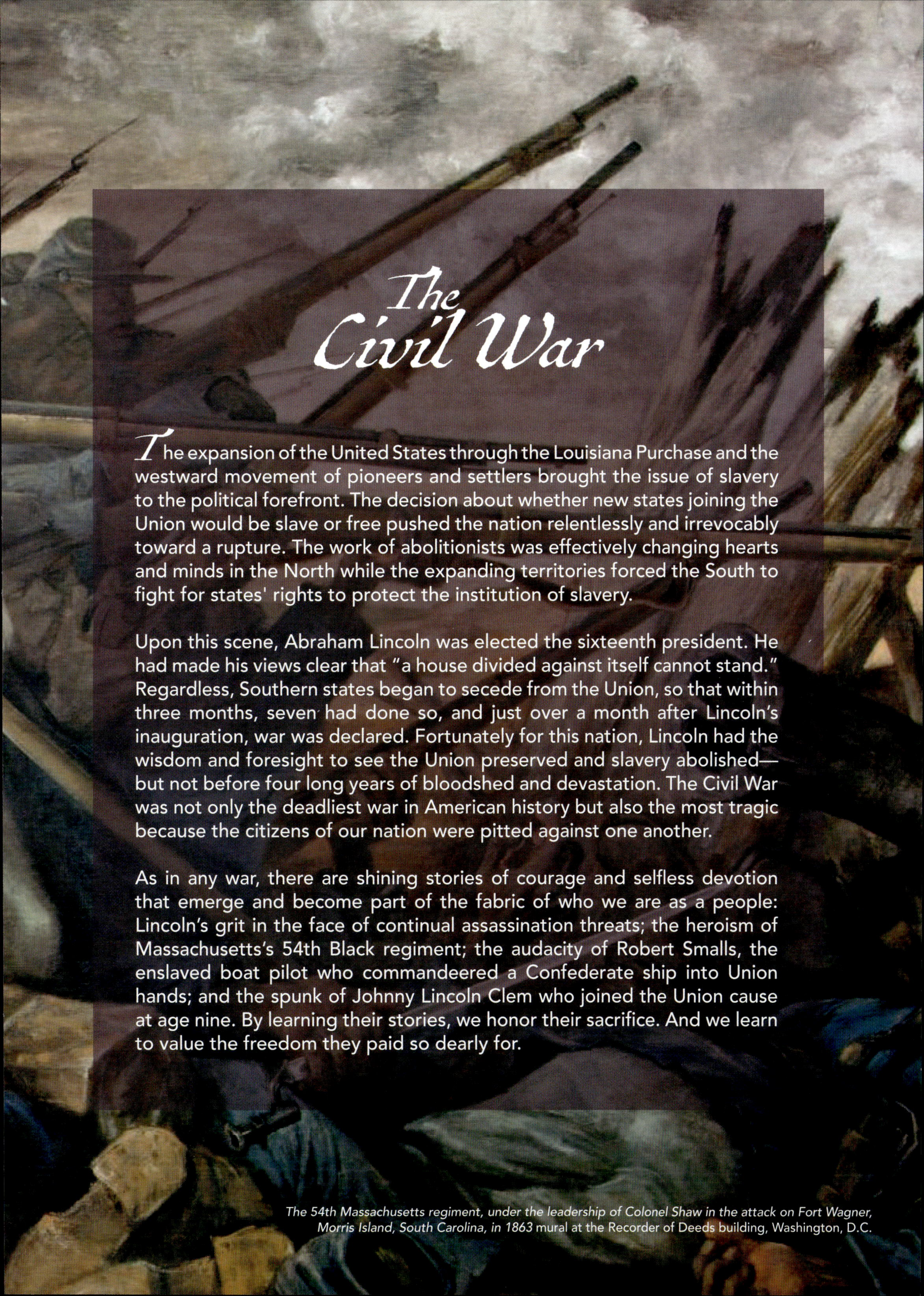

The 54th Massachusetts regiment, under the leadership of Colonel Shaw in the attack on Fort Wagner, Morris Island, South Carolina, in 1863 mural at the Recorder of Deeds building, Washington, D.C.

Rabbit Trails

Fifty Cents and a Dream: Young Booker T. Washington by Jabari Asim
This relates the story of Washington's great passion for education and his 500-mile walk to Hampton Institute where he realizes his dream.

Let It Shine: Stories of Black Women Freedom Fighters by Andrea Davis Pinkney
The anthology features the stories of ten courageous women who worked faithfully and sacrificially to achieve equality, opportunity, and justice by shining their light and raising their voices.

Moses: How Harriet Tubman Led Her People to Freedom by Carole Boston Weatherford
Combining evocative illustrations with a text that focuses on Tubman's deep faith and how God never failed her, this is a beautiful book.

Words Set Me Free: The Story of Young Frederick Douglass by Lesa Cline-Ransome
& *Escape from Slavery: The Boyhood of Frederick Douglass in His Own Words* by Michael McCurdy
Both books tell the gripping story of Douglass's passion for learning, his patient but proactive preparation for freedom, and his eventual escape. The latter title carries the story on through his adult life and his relentless advocacy for abolition.

Bill Pickett: Rodeo-Riding Cowboy by Andrea D. Pinkney
Bill Picket is the tale of one of the most fearless rodeo-riding cowboys of all time. The unknown Texas boy born into slavery became the most famous bulldogging cowboy in the history of rodeo, known and celebrated around the world.

Red Cloud's War by Paul Goble
Amazing illustrations and text tell the story of the Fetterman Fight—the U.S. Army's worst defeat against the Oglala Lakota when the U.S. government demanded their land to build forts and access gold mines.

Henry's Freedom Box by Ellen Levine
This is the true story of the slave Henry Brown who risks his life to mail himself in a crate to freedom. After his wife and children are sold south, Henry no longer wishes to live, until a friend offers to help ship him to freedom.

Pink and Say by Patricia Polacco
The true story of a young black Union soldier, Pinkus, who rescues a wounded comrade left for dead on the battlefield. Pinkus's mother nurses the boy, Say, back to health, but the two boys' presence is putting her in mortal danger. A tender story of kindness and compassion.

So Tall Within by Gary Schmid
The story of Sojourner Truth—the illiterate former slave who walked over thousands of miles preaching eloquently about a woman's right to vote, reforming prisons, and the evils of slavery.

Before She Was Harriet by Lesa-Cline Ransome
A look at the life of Tubman through the numerous roles she played—suffragist, Union spy, general, nurse, conductor, Minty, and Araminta.

John Henry by Julius Lester
The story of the fabled strongman of American folklore who battled against a steam engine in the days when the country was young, and hopes were high.

I'll Pass for Your Comrade: Women Soldiers in the Civil War
by Anita Silvey
It is not a well-known fact that many women, disguised as men, served as soldiers in the Civil War. Their colorful stories are told here in this well-researched and remarkable text.

Looking at Lincoln by Maira Kalman
A loving tribute to the man who kept the Union together and set in motion the emancipation of the slaves in this country. He gave his life for doing so.

A Boy Named Beckoning
& Red Bird Sings: The Story of Zitkala-Ša by Gina Capaldi
Tell the stories of two Native American—one a doctor and the other a musician and writer, who rose above the terrible injustices that were inflicted on Native populations and brought hope and some justice to their beloved people.

Undying Glory: The Story of the Massachusetts 54th Regiment
by Clinton Cox

Massachusetts's 54th Regiment was the first all-Black corps to serve in the Civil War. Made up of Black freemen and escaped slaves, this regiment served so nobly and with such courage that one Union commander said their story "will be forever traced in undying glory." They came from over twenty-two states, Canada, and even Bermuda, and the West Indies. Abraham Lincoln said of them, "Without the help of black freemen, the war against the South could not have been won." The film *Glory*, winner of five Academy Awards, tells the story of this noble regiment but should be previewed before watching with intermediate students. The 1991 documentary film, *Civil War—The True Story of Glory Continues* by Lionheart Filmworks is available on YouTube and is appropriate for middle-grade students.

Crafts & Projects

Civil War Handkerchief Doll

This post provides historical information on handkerchief dolls and instructions on making your own!

http://itssopurdy.blogspot.com/2012/10/how-to-civil-war-handkerchief-dolls.html

Build a Log Cabin Diorama

The nineteenth century was a period of rapid expansion in the United States, and settlers like Abraham Lincoln's family often built log cabins. There are many how-to videos and design ideas online.

Build a Civil War Battle Diorama

For those of you who want to take on a real miniature design challenge, check out Pinterest and YouTube for inspiration and instructions.

Make a Quill Pen

Many people employed quill pens at this time in history. Make your own and try your hand at some traditional script.

www.wikihow.com/Make-a-Quill-Pen-out-of-a-Feather

Character Connection: Kindness

During the worst of times, kindness shines brightest and serves as a beacon of hope. In the stories you are about to read, you will encounter acts of kindness, courage, and love in the worst of national conflicts, civil war. The American Civil War tore the nation in two, threatening its very existence, and set brother against brother. In this ugly time, kindness was more important than ever. Use the following Bible verses to discuss the power of kindness as seen in the following stories.

Proverbs 11:17
Proverbs 31:26
Luke 6:35
Acts 20:35
Galatians 6:10
Ephesians 4:32
Philippians 2:1-30
Colossians 3:12-14
1 Peter 3:9
1 Peter 4:9
1 John 3:18

Online Resources

The American Civil War Museum offers virtual visits, workshops, and other resources: https://acwm.org/learn/homefronted/.

The National Museum of African American History and Culture offers virtual visits, photos of objects made by enslaved Africans in America, and much more: https://nmaahc.si.edu/.

Vox.com features a site titled "37 Maps that explain the Civil War." Many of these maps give visuals to help understand various aspects of the war.

LESSON 118

1. Read Chapters 30-32 of *A Child's First*. These chapters provide the foundation for our next section on the Civil War.

2. Have your student cut out, color, and paste the Pony Express picture on the timeline.

3. Many of the horses used on the rugged western portion of the Pony Express were American mustangs. Cut out the American mustang image from the Picture Packet and have your student color and add it to the notebook along with a few facts from your research.

LESSON 119

1. Introduce *Lincoln: A Photobiography* by Russell Freedman. Read Chapters 1-2.

   a. Abraham Lincoln was described as a "man of many faces." The introductory chapters show how aspects of Abe's personality seemed contradictory to one another. As the author describes Abe's manner, consider what you might have thought of Lincoln if you had been able to meet him. Points for discussion: Abe could be gloomy and depressed, but he also loved to tell jokes. Lincoln seemed to care little for his appearance, yet he bought two suits per year from Springfield's finest tailor. Lincoln had little formal education and mispronounced some words, yet became an eloquent orator and fine writer.

   b. Arthur Conan Doyle once said, "It is easy to be wise after the event." Discuss how to apply this quote to the evolution of Frederick Douglass's opinion of Abraham Lincoln. Discuss how hindsight enabled Douglass to see the "infinite wisdom" Lincoln had in preserving the Union and freeing the slaves.

   c. Discuss why Lincoln desired to study law. *Lincoln was always embarrassed by his lack of formal education and felt that studying law would allow him to rise in the world, earn a respectable place in the community, and live by his wits rather than physical labor.*

2. Have your student begin a new section in the notebook on Lincoln. Copy Frederick Douglass's quote from page 5 of *Lincoln: A Photobiography* into the notebook.

3. Lincoln loved reading, and the books and poetry he enjoyed shaped the man he became. One of his favorite poems was William Knox's *"Mortality."* Read this poem on page 129 of this guide, and discuss how you think it influenced Lincoln. Have your student write out their favorite passage from the poem along with their reflections in the Lincoln section of the notebook.

4. Have your student cut out, color, and paste the Abraham Lincoln picture on the timeline.

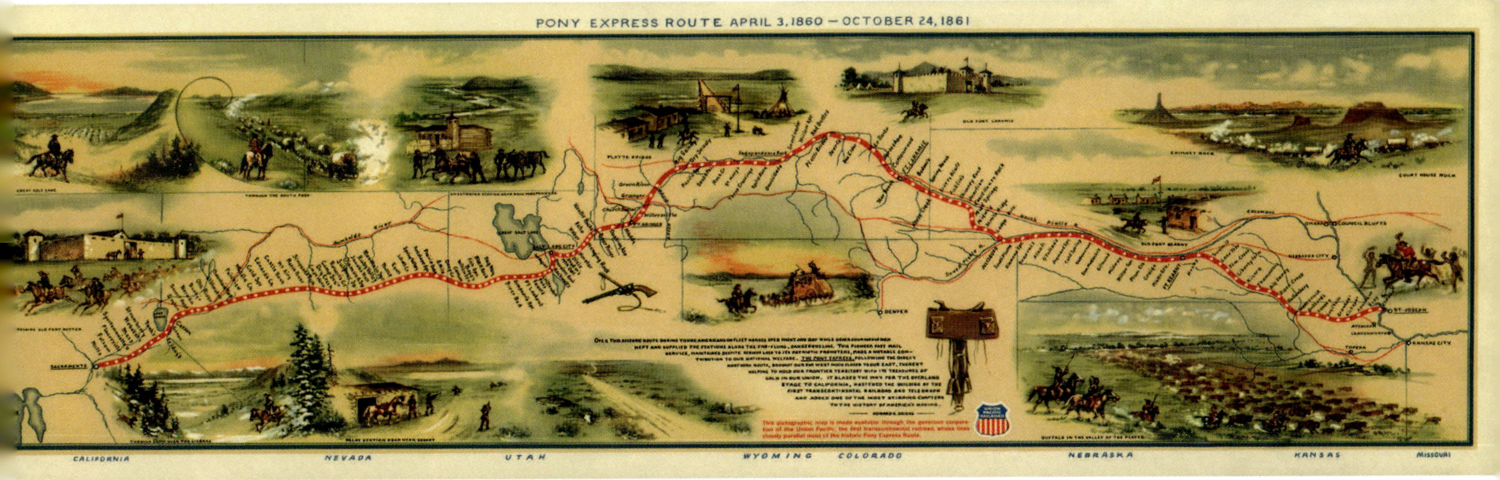

trated Map of Pony Express Route in 1860 by William Henry Jackson

LESSON 120

1. The Missouri Compromise and the Kansas-Nebraska Act were crucial pieces of legislation that tried to deal with the spread of slavery in the U.S. and its territories. To learn more, watch the following videos:
"How one piece of legislation divided a nation–Ben Labaree, Jr." on the TedEd YouTube channel
"The Ultimate Guide to the Presidents: The Civil War & A Nation Divided (1849-1865)" on the History YouTube channel

2. Read Chapters 3-4 of *Lincoln: A Photobiography.*

a. What were the two political parties at this time, and what were their positions on the role of the federal government? To which party did Lincoln belong? *The two parties were Whig and Democrat; the former supported a strong federal government, while Democrats believed in strong state governments free of interference from Washington. Lincoln was a Whig.*

b. How did Lincoln's stand on principle regarding the Mexican War cost him politically? *The Mexican War was a political war designed to grab Mexican territory for the United States. Lincoln's willingness to speak out against it—calling the war "immoral and unnecessary"—cost him his congressional seat.*

c. Why was Lincoln a much-sought-after lawyer? *Lincoln mastered every detail of his cases before going to court, he seasoned his arguments with wit and humor, and he reduced complex issues to simple forms.*

d. Lincoln stated, "It is my pleasure that my children are free, happy, and unrestrained by parental tyranny. Love is the chain whereby to bind a child to its parents." Discuss Lincoln's perspective on parenting and family relationships.

e. How did the passage of the Kansas-Nebraska Act affect Lincoln? *Lincoln was "thunderstruck and stunned," and seeing that slavery would not "die a natural death" compelled him to reenter politics.*

3. Have your student record in the notebook some of Lincoln's statements on page 55 of *Lincoln: A Photobiography* concerning slavery and the Union.

4. Have your student cut out, color, and paste the Civil War picture on the timeline.

LESSON 121

1. Read Chapter 5 of *Lincoln: A Photobiography.* **Note:** Page 88 contains a disturbing photo of war casualties.

a. The U.S. Capitol building was heavily defended during Lincoln's inauguration. In more recent history, defenses were set up for President Biden's inauguration in 2021. Discuss the circumstances surrounding both these events and the similarities and differences. Points of discussion: In both instances, the city was on edge in the weeks leading up to the inaugurations due to rumors, incidents of violence, assassination plots, and the spread of misinformation.

b. After the inauguration, Southern states began to secede from the Union. While Stephen Douglas had been Lincoln's political rival, he showed graciousness when he visited Lincoln at the White House. What is remarkable about his visit? *Though Douglas was pro-slavery, he denounced the rebels who had seceded and offered Lincoln his support in upholding the Union.*

c. Describe some of the challenges Lincoln faced as commander in chief of the armed forces. *Lincoln lacked military experience and had a string of ineffective military commanders who shrank from making decisions and going into battle. Even when the Union forces won a battle, casualties were horrific.*

O why should the spirit of mortal be proud?
Like a fast-flitting meteor, a fast-flying cloud,
A flash of the lightning, a break of the wave,
He passes from life to his rest in the grave.

The leaves of the oak and the willow shall fade,
Be scattered around, and together be laid;
And the young and the old, and the low and the high,
Shall moulder to dust, and together shall lie.

The child that a mother attended and loved,
The mother that infant's affection that proved;
The husband that mother and infant that blessed,
Each, all, are away to their dwelling of rest.

The maid on whose cheek, on whose brow, in whose eye,
Shone beauty and pleasure—her triumphs are by;
And the memory of those that beloved her and praised
Are alike from the minds of the living erased.

The hand of the king that the scepter hath borne,
The brow of the priest that the miter hath worn,
The eye of the sage, and the heart of the brave,
Are hidden and lost in the depths of the grave.

The peasant whose lot was to sow and to reap,
The herdsman who climbed with his goats to the steep,
The beggar that wandered in search of his bread,
Have faded away like the grass that we tread.

The saint that enjoyed the communion of heaven,
The sinner that dared to remain unforgiven,
The wise and the foolish, the guilty and just,
Have quietly mingled their bones in the dust.

So the multitude goes, like the flower and the weed
That wither away to let others succeed;
So the multitude comes, even those we behold,
To repeat every tale that hath often been told.

For we are the same that our fathers have been;
We see the same sights that our fathers have seen,—
We drink the same stream, and we feel the same sun,
And we run the same course that our fathers have run.

The thoughts we are thinking, our fathers would think;
From the death we are shrinking, they too would shrink;
To the life we are clinging to, they too would cling;
But it speeds from the earth like a bird on the wing.

They loved, but the story we cannot unfold;
They scorned, but the heart of the haughty is cold;
They grieved, but no wail from their slumber may come;
They enjoyed, but the voice of their gladness is dumb.

They died, ay! they died! and we things that are now,
Who walk on the turf that lies over their brow,
Who make in their dwellings a transient abode,
Meet the changes they met on their pilgrimage road.

Yea! hope and despondence, and pleasure and pain,
Are mingled together like sunshine and rain;
And the smile and the tear, and the song and the dirge,
Still follow each other, like surge upon surge.

'Tis the wink of an eye, 'tis the draught of a breath,
From the blossom of health to the paleness of death,
From the gilded saloon to the bier and the shroud—
O why should the spirit of mortal be proud?

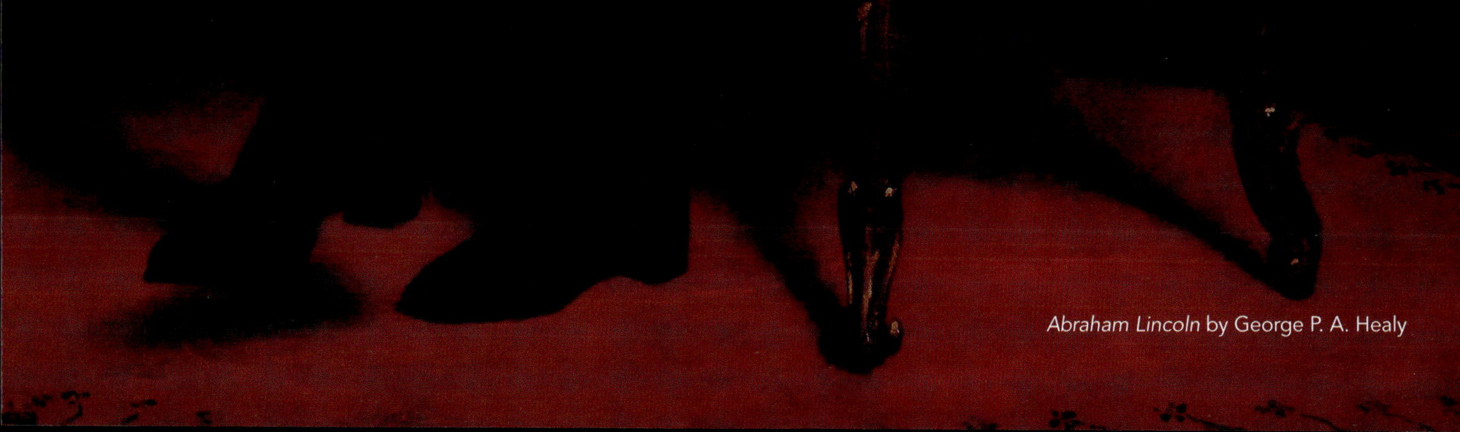

Abraham Lincoln by George P. A. Healy

Good Law Criteria

For a law to qualify as a good law, it must have the following characteristics:

I) The law must be in the interest of the people.

II) The law must not discriminate. This means the law must be applied equally to everybody.

III) A good law must be reasonable; the law should not be too harsh or rigid.

IV) A good law should be made known to the people who are going to be ruled by it.

V) A good law should not suppress the people.

Political cartoon featuring Abraham Lincoln, General McClellan, and Jefferson Davis

Good Law Criteria Source:
https://qknowbooks.gitbooks.io/jhs_2_social_studies-law-and-order-in-our/content/characteristics_of_a_good_law.html

LESSON 121 continued

d. When Republican leaders came to Lincoln during the war, they urged him to free the slaves. They stated that it was absurd to fight the war without destroying the institution that caused it (page 85). Discuss what they meant by this.

e. How did Lincoln solve the problem of emancipation while not offending the slave states that had remained loyal to the Union? What did William H. Seward advise that Lincoln agreed was wise? *Lincoln decided to free only the slaves of the rebel states. Seward advised waiting until the Union forces had a significant victory.*

2. Watch "The Civil War, Part I: Crash Course US History #20" on the CrashCourse YouTube channel. Discuss the advantages the North had over the South at the onset of the war. For specifics, review page 73 of *Lincoln: A Photobiography.*

3. Have your student cut out, color, and paste the Emancipation Proclamation picture on the timeline.

4. Read Chapter 33 of *A Child's First.*

LESSON 122

1. Watch "The Civil War Part 2: Crash Course US History #21" on the CrashCourse YouTube channel.

2. Read Chapters 6-7 of *Lincoln: A Photobiography.* **Note:** Page 100 contains a disturbing photo of war casualties.

a. President Lincoln suffered terrible backlash for emancipating the slaves. How did he respond to his detractors and those who told him to reverse freeing the slaves? *Lincoln said, "I am a slow walker, but I never walk backwards."*

b. Frederick Douglass came to honor and respect Lincoln deeply. What quality of Lincoln did Douglass most admire? *Douglass most admired Lincoln's "entire freedom from popular prejudice against the colored race."*

c. Study the political cartoon on page 110 of *Lincoln: A Photobiography.* Have the student identify each character, what they're fighting over, and how they believe they can save the Union. From the Picture Packet, have the student cut out, color, and paste this cartoon in the notebook along with an explanation of the comic.

d. The day Lincoln was assassinated, he expressed something to his wife that he hadn't said in a long time. What was it? Describe the reasons why Lincoln felt the way he did. *Lincoln told Mary, "I never felt so happy in my life." Lincoln had successfully brought the Civil War to an end. He had preserved the Union, and he had abolished slavery in America. Everything he had worked, prayed, and agonized over had come to pass. He had finished his work.*

e. The day Lincoln was assassinated is one of the most noted religious days of the year. What is it? *Lincoln was assassinated on Good Friday, just one week after the war was over.*

3. Read the criteria for a good law in the sidebar. Look up the 13th Amendment and evaluate and discuss the amendment based upon these criteria.

4. Have your student cut out, color, and paste the 13th Amendment picture on the timeline.

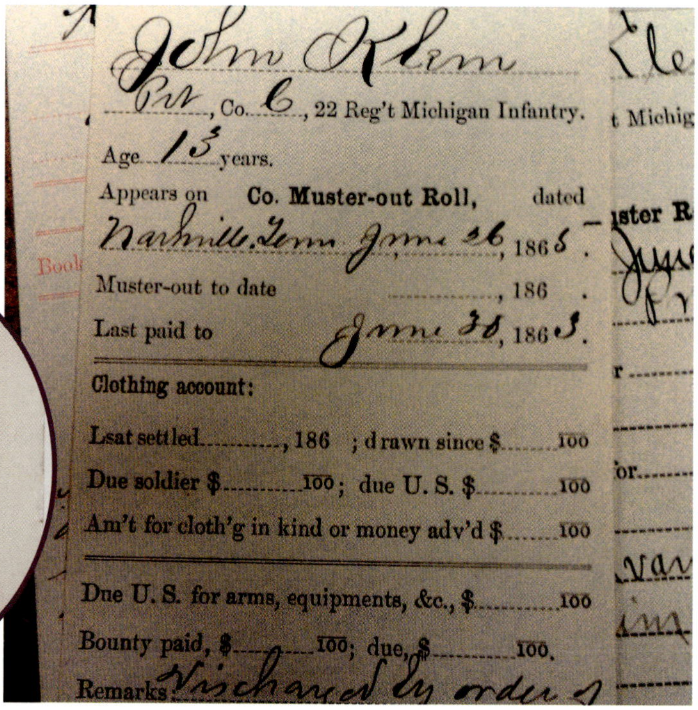

John Klem
Pvt, Co. C, 22 Reg't Michigan Infantry.
Age 13 years.
Appears on Co. Muster-out Roll, dated
Nashville, Tenn June 26, 1865.
Muster-out to date ......, 186 .
Last paid to June 30, 1863.
Clothing account:
Lsat settled ...., 186 ; drawn since $ 100
Due soldier $ .... 100; due U. S. $ 100
Am't for cloth'g in kind or money adv'd $ 100
Due U. S. for arms, equipments, &c., $ 100
Bounty paid, $ .... 100; due, $ .... 100.
Remarks: Discharged by order of

1. John Lincoln Clem. 2. Enlistment papers of John Lincoln Clem (spelled Klem here).
3. Painting titled *Come and Join Us Brothers* by the Supervisory Committee For Recruiting Colored Regiments.

LESSON 123

1. We will now read about the experiences of the youngest person to serve in the Union Army during the Civil War. Introduce *John Lincoln Clem: Civil War Drummer Boy*. This book tells the true story of John Lincoln Clem, a boy who ran away to serve in the Union Army when he was nine years old. Johnny is brave, willful, and feisty, and this comes through in the story, so there are some instances of disrespectful talk and actions, but they are true to Johnny's nature. For historical context, read the Historical Note starting on page 170 of *John Lincoln Clem*. Read Chapters 1-3. Discussion prompts:

a. History tends to flatten personalities and create formal dialogue. This book preserves the color and flavor of how real people spoke. Does anything about the dialogue surprise you? Do you think it's authentic? Why or why not? When someone living 200 years from now watches a recording of how we speak today, what do you think they will find surprising?

b. Why did Johnny hate trains? *Johnny hated trains because his mother had been killed by one.*

c. Discuss Johnny's decision to run away to join the Union Army. Do you think he was foolish, courageous, rebellious, or all the above? Why? Did he think about how his actions would affect his family when he decided to leave without telling anyone?

d. Discuss how Johnny was motivated by the love of his country to join the Third Ohio. What threat did the United States face at this time? *The United States was divided as never before. Abraham Lincoln's election had forced the issue of slavery, and the Southern states had seceded.*

2. Over the next week, have your student write a brief report on Abraham Lincoln's life and the key reasons he is still considered the most beloved president in American history. Intersperse within the report some of Lincoln's memorable sayings. To conclude the essay, copy the passage from Lincoln's Second Inaugural Address on page 113 of *Lincoln: A Photobiography* into the notebook.

LESSON 124

1. Read Chapters 4-6 of *John Lincoln Clem*.

a. In Chapter 4, William told Johnny to start thinking about his time in the Army "as a job." Johnny was not officially enlisted and, therefore, was unpaid. Discuss William and Johnny's differing motivations for joining the army.

b. Johnny experienced battle for the first time in Chapter 5. Narrate his experience. Discuss why Johnny felt like he let down his fellow soldiers. Although Johnny was only nine years old at the time, he had volunteered for an important job and was expected to follow commands. Discuss how children are affected by war.

c. Discuss Captain McDougal's reason for refusing to accept William's argument that Jackson must be returned: "That was a law enforced by states that no longer want to be a part of this Union. Those laws no longer apply to us." To which law do you think William and McDougal were referring? *The Fugitive Slave Act.*

2. For hundreds of years, drummers were the communication channels of armies. They communicated orders, movements, and inspiration to the soldiers efficiently. Refer to the glossary beginning on page 179 of *John Lincoln Clem* to learn more about each drum call. To hear examples of what these calls sounded like, watch "The Civil War: Drum Commands" on the Ethan Mayo YouTube channel.

LESSON 125

1. Read Chapters 7-9 of *John Lincoln Clem.*

 a. On page 58, Johnny thinks, "Funny how you can agree with a fella and still disagree with him." Discuss how this thought related to William's scar. How did Johnny both agree and disagree with William? Can you think of an instance where you've agreed and disagreed with someone?

 b. The pig that Johnny killed fed his regiment, and even the general enjoyed it! Why was Johnny still punished for killing it? Discuss the importance of discipline and obeying orders in the military. *Johnny killed the pig in direct violation of the Union soldiers' orders to leave civilians and their property alone. So even though everyone enjoyed the pork roast, Johnny had to be punished so that other soldiers would not start raiding civilian farms and homes. Armies depend on immediate and unquestioned obedience to maintain the order necessary to do what armies are supposed to do—fight.*

 c. Earlier, you discussed Johnny and William's differing motivations for fighting in this war. Why was Jackson fighting? *Jackson was motivated by the idea that his little brother could be free.*

2. The reasons for the Civil War are still debated to this day, and the most helpful resources for learning more are primary sources. These are artifacts, documents, diary entries, manuscripts, autobiographies, recordings, or any other source of information created at the time being studied or discussed. To understand the Confederacy's perspective, one must read the primary sources. One excellent source is the official Declarations of Causes put forth by the various Southern states. Access these statements at the following link, read one or two statements with your student, and discuss: www.battlefields.org/learn/primary-sources/declaration-causes-seceding-states

LESSON 126

1. Read Chapters 10-13 of *John Lincoln Clem.*

 a. These chapters introduce war. What aspects did you find most surprising? Discuss Harry's desertion.

 b. When the Union soldiers raided the house of the elderly Confederate, what did Johnny realize? What do you think he meant by it? *Johnny realized, "This is everybody's war, not just soldiers."*

 c. Discuss how Jackson's experience of being a drummer boy was different from Johnny's. Did Jackson find the camaraderie and brotherhood that Johnny had with the Third Ohio? Why do you think their experiences were so different?

2. The Battle of Shiloh marked a turning point in the Civil War. If your student is a fan of military history, watch "Battle of Shiloh (1862) – American Civil War DOCUMENTARY" on the Kings and Generals YouTube channel.

3. The Seventy-Ninth Colored was one of the first Black units to see combat in the Civil War. Read more about this historic and courageous unit here: https://civilwaronthewesternborder.org/encyclopedia/1st-kansas-colored-volunteers-later-79th-us-colored-infantry

LESSON 127

1. Read Chapters 14-17 of *John Lincoln Clem.*

 a. Why did Johnny leave the Third Ohio? *A soldier from the Twenty-Second Michigan offered him an enlistment and the opportunity to be a hero, something close to Johnny's heart.*

2. Read Chapter 34 of *A Child's First.* Although some of this information will be repetitive, it will also fill in Generals Grant and Sherman's military strategy and touch on the Southern perspective.

LESSON 128

1. Finish reading *John Lincoln Clem.*

a. At the beginning of the story, Johnny was an angry, grieving, defiant, spirited boy of nine years old. By the time he became a prisoner of war in Georgia, he had grown in years, maturity, and character. Discuss the following: How had Johnny changed throughout the story? Did he still long to be a hero? How did he come to accept that being "a kid" had advantages?

b. Discuss Johnny's reunion with his family. What stood out to you?

c. Johnny clearly felt the tremendous cost of the Civil War during his time in the Union Army. How did Elijah's surprise visit demonstrate the worthiness of this war? *Elijah was free. Jackson's dream for his brother was a reality, and Jackson had paid the ultimate price in the fight for his brother's freedom.*

LESSON 129

1. John Lincoln Clem's story shows that the Civil War was fought by ordinary people who answered a difficult call. We have seen that soldiers' motives varied from earning a wage to patriotic belief in the Union to a desire to end slavery. We will conclude our study with the remarkable story of an enslaved man who risked everything to gain freedom for his family while courageously executing a daring act to benefit the Union. Read *Seven Miles to Freedom: The Robert Smalls Story.*

2. To learn more about the remarkable life of Robert Smalls, watch the following talk given by his great-great-grandson, Michael B. Moore:
"'The Audacity of Robert Smalls' | Michael B. Moore | TEDxStMarksSchool" on the TEDx Talks channel.

3. Reflect with your student on the historical adventure you've now completed. Which stories stand out? Why? At the very beginning, you discussed the ideals outlined on pages 8-9 of *A Child's First.* Let's return to that discussion. How has your understanding of those ideals expanded? What sacrifices were made in support of these essential principles? How has the United States engaged in an "unending struggle for social justice"? When has our nation fulfilled those highest ideals, and when has she failed to live up to them? As you think about your nation's history, what lessons have you learned from the people who came before you? Have your student record their thoughts in the notebook.

Robert Smalls, the Civil War hero, was born a slave in a cabin at the back of this property in Beaufort, South Carolina. After the war, he returned to Beaufort and purchased this home where he'd previously been enslaved.

Historic Table

Crab Croquettes

What Mrs. Fisher Knows About Southern Cooking was a cookbook published in 1881 by Abby Fisher, a former slave. Fisher moved from South Carolina to San Francisco in 1877, where she established a catering business and made award-winning pickles and preserves. Though Fisher was illiterate, her patrons convinced her to publish her recipes, which she dictated. Her cookbook is one of the first cookbooks published by an African American woman. You can read her full cookbook online. I have adapted her crab cake recipe for modern cooks.

1 pound Dungeness crab, chopped in chunks
1/3 cup grated celery (squeeze out excess moisture)
2 tablespoons finely chopped sweet onion
1/3 cup mayonnaise
1 cup crushed Ritz crackers
1 teaspoon Old Bay seasoning
A few dashes Tabasco (to taste)
2 tablespoons chopped fresh parsley
2 eggs
Lard (or butter) for frying

Squeeze excess moisture from crab with a paper towel. Add half the cracker crumbs and the rest of the ingredients except the eggs. Mix well and form into patties. Beat two eggs, dip croquettes in the egg, roll in powdered crackers before frying; have your lard hot, and fry just before wanted at the table. Serve immediately with lemon and tartar sauce. Coleslaw and corn on the cob make nice side dishes to crab cakes.

Abe Lincoln's Favorite Almond Cake

Mary Todd made this cake for Lincoln when they were courting, and it became one of his regular favorites. Notice there is no leavening, as it was not available until the late 1860s.

1/2 cup (8 tablespoons) butter, melted
1/4 cup crème fraîche (or sour cream)
1 cup sugar
2 eggs
1 cup sifted all-purpose flour
1/2 cup almond flour
1 pinch salt
1 teaspoon almond extract
1/3 cup sliced or slivered almonds, toasted
Powdered sugar to dust cake

Preheat the oven to 350°F. Combine the butter, crème fraîche, and sugar, and mix until well-combined. Add the eggs one at a time, mixing until well-incorporated. Add the flours, salt, and almond extract. Mix well and then pour into a greased tarte or cake pan. Shower the cake with almonds. Bake for 25 to 35 minutes, until golden brown. Let the cake cool slightly. Dust with powdered sugar. If desired, top with lightly sweetened whipped cream. Lingonberry jam makes a wonderful topping too.

In Conclusion

As we have moved through the early history of our nation, we have learned about the great principles that guided those who walked before us. From the ideals of the Iroquois' Great Rule of Peace and the Mayflower Compact to the values proclaimed in the Declaration of Independence and U.S. Constitution, we can see the best of our history. We have also seen the lowest points where these principles were not just ignored but blatantly violated. This should not surprise us because history is the story of people, and people are complex, flawed, and capable of greatness and great evil. History is most useful when it shows us what we can aspire to and what we ought to avoid or correct. When students complete this study, we hope that they will hold in honor those heroic individuals who sacrificed for the good of our country, that they will understand the basic foundations of civil and religious liberty unique to America's founding, and that they will be able to celebrate the rich mosaic of people who contributed to the founding and development of this nation. We hope that learning about both the triumphs and the tragedies will cultivate a desire to be part of our nation's continued striving toward a "more perfect union" for all.

Image Credits

Mesa Verde National Park photo by Alec Krum on Unsplash

Ball-play of the Choctaw by George Catlin, Public domain, via Wikimedia Commons

Early Localization of Native Americans USGS, Public domain, via Wikimedia Commons

Summer Night off the Coast of Greenland by Carl Rasmussen, c. 1000, Public domain, via Wikimedia Commons

1. Bloodofox, CC BY-SA 3.0 <https://creativecommons.org/licenses/by-sa/3.0>, via Wikimedia Commons
2. Codex Runicus, Template:Asztalos Gyula, Public domain, via Wikimedia Commons
3. Scandinavian settlement, Max Naylor, Public domain, via Wikimedia Commons

1. Iroquois Nations Map, R. A. Nonenmacher, Public domain, via Wikimedia Commons
2. By Reproduction of an older original Iroquois painting. - Alexander, Hartley Burr, Public domain, via Wikimedia Commons

1. Four Mohawk Kings painted by Jan Verelst, 1720, Public domain, via Wikimedia Commons
2. *Ball Players* by George Catlin, Public Domain, via Wikimedia Commons

Landing of Columbus by John Vanderlyn, 1847, Public domain, via Wikimedia Commons

Christopher Columbus at the gates of the monastery of Santa Maria de la Rabida with his son Diego by Benito Mercade y Fabrega, 1858, Public domain, via Wikimedia Commons

1. Sculpture by Taíno, Walters Art Museum, Publi domain, via Wikimedia Commons
2. Photo by Angel Ceballos on Unsplash
3. *Columbus's Voyages* By Viajes_de_colon.svg: Phirosiberiaderivative work: Phirosiberia (talk) - Viajes_de_colon.svg, CC BY-SA 3.0, https://commons.wikimedia.org/w/index.php?curid=8849049

The Mayflower Compact by N. C. Wyeth, 1938, Public domain

Coming of the Mayflower by N. C. Wyeth, 1941

1. *The Coronation of Powhatan* by John Gadsby Chapman, Public Domain, https://commons.wikimedia.org/w/index.php?curid=10183926
2. National Archives at College Park, Public domain, via Wikimedia Commons

Panorama of London by Claes Van Visscher, 1616, Public domain, via Wikimedia Commons

1. Geneva Bible printed in Amsterdam in 1633, Public domain, via Wikimedia Commons
2. By Hi540 - Own work, CC BY-SA 4.0, https://commons.wikimedia.org/w/index.php?curid=3226868

1. Samoset appears at Plymouth engraving, Public domain, via Wikimedia Commons
2. "Massasoit, Great Sachem of the Wampanoag, Friend and Protector of the Pilgrims, 1621" scuplture by Cyrus E. Dallin in Kansas City, Missouri, Public domain, via Wikimedia Commons
3. *The Departure of the Mayflower* by N.C. Wyeth, 1941, Public domain, via Wikimedia Commons

18th-century map of Philadelphia, circa 1752, Public Domain, via Wikimedia Commons

1. Seal of the State of Pennsylvania
2. Statue of William Penn, Adobe Stock
3. Statue of Tamanend in Philadelphia, Photo Alec Rogers © 2016 for the Association for Public Art
4. *Penn's Treaty with the Indians at Shackamaxon* by Benjamin West - Pennsylvania Academy of Fine Arts, Philadelphia, Public Domain, https://commons.wikimedia.org/w/index.php?curid=817244

Detailed Triangle Trade, Image by Supportstorm, via Wikimedia Commons

Map of the French and Indian War: By Hoodinski - Own work, CC BY-SA 3.0, via Wikimedia Commons

Battle of Long Island by Domenick D'Andrea, Public domain, via Wikimedia Commons

1. *Poems on Various Subjects, Religious and Moral* by Phillis Wheatley, engraving attributed to Scipio Moorhead, 1773, Public domain
2. Abolitionist woodcarvings used by the Society for the Abolition of Slavery in England, Public domain

The Boston Tea Party by John Andrews, 1856, Public domain

Boston Massacre by Paul Revere, based on earlier engraving by Harry Pelham, 1770, Public domain

1. *Advance of the Enemy* by Alfred Wordsworth Thompson, Public domain, via Wikimedia Commons
2. *Pulling Down the Statue of King George III, New York City* by Johannes Adam Simon Oertel, Public domain, via Wikimedia Commons

1. *Battle of Guildord Court House* by H. Charles McBarron, Public domain, via Wikimedia Commons
2. The National Guard/Flickr/Public Domain

1. *Abigail Adams* by Benjamin Public Domain, via Wikimedia Commons
2. By Thomas Jefferson, Public Domain, via Wikimedia Commons
3. Peacefield by Daderot, CC BY-SA 3.0, https://commons.wikimedia.org/w/index.php?curid=3162095

The Oregon Trail by Albert Bierstadt, 1869, Public Domain, via Wikiart

1. Chinook Mother and Child by Paul Kane, 1848, Public domain, via Wikimedia Commons
2. Mandan Chief Sheheke, Public Domain, https://commons.wikimedia.org/w/index.php?curid=66572015
3. *The Scouts* by Charles M. Russell, Public domain, via Wikiart

1. Captain Whitfield, Public domain, via Wikimedia Commons
2. *Lancing a Sperm Whale* by Clifford Ashley, 1906, Public domain

1. *The Fugitive Slaves* by Eastman Johnson, Public domain, via Wikimedia Commons
2. Map showing routes on the Underground Railroad, Public domain, via Wikimedia Commons
3. Harriet Tubman, Public domain, via Wikimedia Commons

The Repatriation of the Captives by Hale Woodruff, 1943, Public art

The 54th Massachusetts regiment, under the leadership of Colonel Shaw in the attack on Fort Wagner, Morris Island, South Carolina, in 1863 mural at the Recorder of Deeds building, built in 1943. 515 D St., NW, Washington, D.C., Public domain, via Library of Congress Commons

Illustrated Map of Pony Express Route in 1860 by William Henry Jackson, Public domain, via Wikimedia Commons

Abraham Lincoln by George P.A. Healy (1813 - 1894), Public domain, https://commons.wikimedia.org/w/index.php?curid=21881917

The True Issue or "That's What's the Matter" political cartoon, 1964, Public domain
Good Law Criteria Source:
https://qknowbooks.gitbooks.io/jhs_2_social_studies-law-and-order-in-our/content/characteristics_of_a_good_law.html

1. John Lincoln Clem, photographer unknown, Public domain, via Wikimedia Commons
2. Enlistment papers of John Lincoln Clem (spelled Klem here)
3. *Come and Join Us Brothers* by the Supervisory Committee For Recruiting Colored Regiments, Public domain, via Wikimedia Commons

Robert Smalls, Public domain, via Wikimedia Commons
Robert Smalls house photo by Rea Berg

Statue of Liberty by Luke Stackpoole on Unsplash